THE LAST WOLF

THE LAST WOLF

Jim Crumley

BIRLINN

First published in 2010 by
Birlinn Limited
West Newington House
10 Newington Road
Edinburgh
EH9 1QS

www.birlinn.co.uk

ISBN: 978 1 84158 847 6

British Library Cataloguing-in-Publication Data
A catalogue record for this book is available from the
British Library

Typeset in Sabon at Birlinn

Printed and bound in Great Britain by
CPI Cox & Wyman, Reading

CONTENTS

v

ACKNOWLEDGEMENTS

The author gratefully acknowledges a grant from the Society of Authors that greatly assisted the cause of this work.

Thanks to the publishers of the following works for permission to quote from them in the text:

Decade of the Wolf by Douglas Smith and Gary Ferguson, Lyons Press, 2005

Comeback Wolves edited by Gary Wockner, Gregory McNamee and SueEllen Campbell, Johnson Books, 2005

Wolfsong by Catherine Feher-Elston, 2004

On the Crofters' Trail by David Craig, Cape, 1990

Of Wolves and Men by Barry Lopez, Touchstone, 1978

The Wolf by Erik Zimen, Souvenir Press, 1981

The Company of Wolves by Peter Steinhart, Vintage, 1996

The author is also grateful to the late Aldo Leopold (*A Sand County Almanac*), Margiad Evans (*Autobiography*) and Seton Gordon (*The Charm of Skye*) for books which had a profound influence on his life and work, and to J.E. Harting (*British Animals Extinct Within Historic Times*) whose book did no such thing, but without which this book would have been much tougher to write.

Particular thanks to my friend and landscape painter of distinction, Sherry Palmer of New Hampshire, for choice examples of American wolf literature and for countless cuttings of American journalism on the subject of wolves; and to Molly Pickall and Sarah Deopsomer of the Yellowstone Wolf Project who were extremely helpful and encouraging.

Of all the native biological constituents of a northern wilderness scene, I should say that the wolves present the greatest test of human wisdom and good intentions.

– Paul Errington, *Of Predation and Life* (1967)

PROLOGUE

The Painter of Mountains

THE THING about the mountain after the wolves came was that it started to change colour. We noticed the change the second year, in the spring. All along the level shelf at the foot of the screes where the deer used to gather in the evening there was a strange haze. We had never seen that haze before. It was pale green and it floated an inch or two above the ground, a low-lying, pale green mist.

We had only ever seen the red deer there, deer by the hundred, deer browsing the land to a grey-brown all-but-bareness, all-but-bare and all-but-dead. It is, we thought, what deer do. They gathered in the places that sheltered them, places that accommodated their safety-in-numbers temperament. And every morning, once the sun had warmed the mountain, they climbed to higher pastures. They commuted up and down the mountain. But their days routinely ended browsing the level shelf to the bone, to the almost-death of the grasses, mosses, lichens, flowers. When there was nothing left to eat they moved. But as soon as new growth began they returned because they liked the comfort of the shelf under the screes, and the browsing to almost-death resumed. In the long wolfless decades they forgot how to behave like deer. Then the wolves came back, and overnight they remembered.

We looked out one evening and there were no deer. None. We scoured the lower slopes, all the ways we knew the deer came down the mountain in the evening. Nothing.

We saw no deer for weeks without knowing why, until on the stillest of evenings a wolf howled. We had never heard a wolf howl. Not even the oldest folk in the glen held the memory of wolves, only the handed-down stories that grew out of an old darkness. That howl, when it came, when it sidled round the mountain edge the way a new-born breeze stirs mist out of stillness, when it stirred things in us we could not name because we had no words for what we had never felt and never known . . . that howl sounded a new beginning for everything in the glen that lived. Everything that lived, breathed, ran, flapped, flew, flowered – and all of us – were changed from that moment.

And in the spring of the second year after the wolves came, we saw the mountain start to change colour. Where the deer had been, where they smothered – suffocated – the growth, bit and bit again the heather-high trees (twenty years old, twenty inches high and going nowhere until at last they were bitten to death) . . . in that second spring we saw the evening sun illuminate a green haze, low on the land. At first we didn't understand its meaning, so we climbed from the floor of the glen to the old deer terrace, and we found its meaning: fresh, sweet, young, vivid, green grass. The wolves, by keeping the deer constantly on the move, had restored to the mountain a lost meadow.

And as the spring advanced, flowers! Splashes of white and yellow and blue, and the grass ankle-deep.

And with every new season after that, the new growth summoned others to the change: butterflies, moths, berries, berry-and-butterfly-eating birds; then the first new trees.

It has been ten years since the wolves came back. Their howls have become the mountain's anthem. The deer still come back to the old terrace, of course, but in much smaller groups, and only for a few days at a time. Then they vanish, and we know they have moved on to the rhythm demanded of them by the wolves. The trees are many, and tall, taller than the biggest stag. The oldest memories in the glen do not remember trees before.

Now, every year at the first hint of spring, we watch the low sun in the evening for the first illumination of the new green mist.

The wolf that was handed down from the old darkness was a slayer of babies, a robber of graves, and a despoiler of the battlefield dead. The wolf that howls in our dusk is a painter of mountains.

THE LAST WOLF

CHAPTER 1
False Wolves and True

Clearly, this is an animal less likely to offer
scientists irrefutable facts than to lure us on a
long and crooked journey of constant learning.
  – Douglas W. Smith and Gary Ferguson,
      Decade of the Wolf (2005)

I MET A MAN in Norway who told me this true story:
'A friend calls me one Saturday morning . . . he has sled
dogs, and in the night these dogs had been very upset
and made much noises. He was going out to shout at
the dogs, and he doesn't have nothing on him, and it
was winter. And he was standing there shouting at the
dogs and then they were quiet. And when they were
quiet he heard a concert from wolves 200 metres from
his house. And he was standing there pure naked. Can
you imagine that feeling? Nothing on you!'

I said, 'That's got to be the ultimate wilderness
experience.'

My Norwegian friend said, 'Yeah, he thought so
too!'

Ah, but then the story grew legs, became what the
Norwegians call 'a walking story'. My friend heard
it again two weeks later from a completely different

source. The 'concert from wolves' at 200 metres had become a slavering pack that confronted the man and threatened him so that he had to drive them off, and was lucky to escape with his life.

'That was in 14 days,' he said. 'What about 140 days? Or 140 years?'

The process of wolf-legend-making is far from extinct, but that is what happens with some people and wolves. The truth is never enough for them. The man who told me this story is a wildlife photographer and film-maker. He and a friend had just completed a TV film about a pack of wolves that had taken eight years to make. That particular pack's territory is around 1,000 square miles. They find the wolves by tracking them in the winter when the pack uses frozen rivers and lakes as highways and the wolves write their story in the snow. The film-makers read other clues, such as the behaviour of ravens; ravens are forever leading them to wolf kills.

'Tell Jim how many ravens you saw on one wolf-killed moose,' one Norwegian film-maker urged the other.

'Seventy,' he said, and to make sure I had understood his heavily-accented English he elaborated: 'Seven times ten.'

Both men were openly hostile towards biologists who fit radio collars and transmitters to wolves after first firing tranquilliser darts into them from planes or helicopters so the collars and transmitters can be fitted. They raged against the stress the darting causes the wolves. One said: 'The uncollared wolves are the real wild wolves. These people who use the radio collaring

. . . it seems to be the wolves are only things. It's like a computer game.'

I smiled and told them of Aldo Leopold's observation in his timeless landmark in the literature of the natural world, *A Sand County Almanac*: 'Most books of nature writing never mention the wind because they are written behind stoves.'

They smiled back. 'It's the same thing! And it's very exciting to not know everything. If you know everything, it's not exciting.'

The Norwegian Government permits four wolf packs in the country. When I met the film-makers, three out of the four packs, and all the packs in neighbouring Sweden, were collared and tracked by computer. The film-makers were fighting a rearguard action on behalf of the Koppang pack, the one they had filmed. They spoke about the need to allow the wolf to retain its mysteries. Their language surprised me, because, historically, Scandinavians have not made the wolf welcome, and here they were using the kind of language I associate with indigenous North Americans. I liked them because they spoke my language too, and because historically, Scots did not make the wolf welcome either.

I mention all this because in any exploration of the wolf in Scotland, sooner or later someone somewhere will ask you to believe that the last wolf in Scotland – in all Britain, for that matter – was killed in the valley of the River Findhorn south-east of Inverness, around 1743. You will also be asked to believe that the history-making wolf-slayer was a MacQueen, a stalker and a man of giant stature. He would be. Wolf legend is no place for Davids, only Goliaths.

He was six feet seven inches. There's a coincidence – the same height as Scotland's greatest historical hero, William Wallace, or at least the same height as William Wallace's legend has grown to in the 700 years since he died. Like Wallace, MacQueen was possessed of extraordinary powers of strength and courage; and in addition he had 'the best deer hounds in the country'. Well, he would have. You would expect nothing less. The wolf he killed (with his dirk and his bare hands) was huge and black. Well, it would be, you would expect nothing less. And it had killed two children as they crossed the hills accompanied only by their mother. What, only two? When the story was first published in 1830, the Victorians swallowed it whole, in the grand tradition of wolf stories.

And here's another coincidence. At the same time, the Victorians were high on a heady cocktail of Scottish history and Sir Walter Scott, and in that frame of mind, were in the throes of building an extraordinary national monument to one of the greatest figures in any rational assessment of Scottish history – William Wallace. His monument stands on a hilltop on the edge of Stirling within sight of the scene of his finest hour, the Battle of Stirling Bridge in 1297. The coat of arms of the old royal burgh of Stirling was a wolf.

The Victorians loved the story of MacQueen as much as they loathed anything with claws, teeth and hooked beaks. Killing nature's creatures (and often stuffing the results and displaying them in glass cases or on the walls of castles and great houses) was a national pastime among the gun-toting classes. It occurred to no-one that the last wolf in Scotland might not have been killed by a man; nor that it might have died old and alone in a cave, perhaps in the vast wild embrace of Rannoch Moor in the Central Highlands, or in the empty Flow Country of the far north, and many years after any human being last saw a wolf. No-one challenged the evidence on which the story of MacQueen and his casual heroics was hung and presented as fact. But that is what you are up against when you consider the place of the wolf in my country, and for that matter, in so many other countries. That is what I am up against in this book. But first, here is a glimpse of the animal we are talking about: not a supposed-to-be wolf but a real wolf.

She was known as number 14 and her mate was Old Blue. Even if it does sound like the first line of a bad country and western song, it was a match made in heaven, or at least in Yellowstone, which in wolf terms is much the same thing. Biologists like Douglas Smith who are deeply embedded in the project to restore wolves to Yellowstone National Park in the northern United States give wolves numbers or, very occasionally, names, to help keep track of them. Number 14 and Old Blue were two remarkable animals, even by the rarefied standards of the tribe of wild wolves. The average lifespan of a Yellowstone wolf is three to four years. Old Blue was almost 12 when he died, at which point Number 14 had to be at least eight years younger. She learned prodigiously from such a seen-it-all-before wolf as Old Blue, so that when he died, she was equipped for anything that the North American wilderness could throw at her. But first she did something astonishing.

In the last few months of his life, Old Blue and number 14 mated one last time. But when he died, number 14 took off, leaving behind her pups and yearling wolves, leaving the territory of the pack. Alpha female wolves don't take off when they have pups, don't abandon their families. It doesn't happen. But 14 took off alone into deep snow, into a landscape that according to Smith, was 'so inhospitable it contained not a single track of another animal'.

She was eventually found by a spotting plane, gave it a single cold stare, then simply continued travelling until all efforts at tracking her failed. She vanished.

She was gone for a week. Then quite suddenly she turned up again, rejoined her family and the rest of the pack. Smith wrote: 'Though no-one wanted to say 14 travelled alone so far because she was mourning the loss of her mate, some of us privately wondered.'

Travel is the wolf's natural habitat. With no alpha male, but possessed of all the experience and survival skills of Old Blue, number 14 waited for the elk migration to come down from the high ground, then led her pack away, following the elk. Their travels took them into the neighbouring wolf pack territory and into a battle. They killed the resident alpha male and some of the others fled; two died in a snow avalanche. These were found the following summer, 'their skeletons at the foot of a small waterfall, shrouded in the lavender blooms of harebell'.

Number 14's audacious move shook up the established order in that part of Yellowstone, and her pack acquired a huge territory with a single battle, no casualties and no alpha male. But the new territory was harsh in winter, the elk all but vanished, and the pack would have to rely on the formidable prey of bison. At first they travelled further into the National Elk Refuge, but then, and for reasons no-one understood, she led the way back to her hard-won heartland and stayed there, as uncompromising in the life she chose to lead as the territory she won for her pack.

Number 14 was found dead at the age of six, but even her death had something of an aura about it. When national park staff found her, there was a golden eagle on her carcase, and if you like your appreciation of nature well garnished with symbolism, what more do you need than that? The carcase of a moose lay nearby. It seems that an epic encounter had killed both prey and predator. Later observation of the spot revealed a grizzly bear covering her carcase as if it was the bear's own kill. There are no memorials to wolves like these, no epitaphs or eulogies. They live and die at the cutting edge of nature. The death of Number 14 was attended by golden eagle and grizzly bear, and it may be she was mourned by her own kind. Nature marked her passing in a way that honoured her astounding life.

The reintroduction of wolves into Yellowstone in 1995 after an absence of 70 years has been well documented; the lives of many individual wolves have sprung into sharp focus, and their stories have travelled the world. Yet despite these years of precious discovery, despite the sum of accumulated knowledge of earlier wolf biologists and nature writers, and despite the best of twenty-first-century technology, wolves are forever baffling and outwitting our own species. We simply don't know why they do certain things. 'Clearly,' wrote

Smith and Ferguson in *Decade of the Wolf,* 'this is an animal less likely to offer scientists irrefutable facts than to lure us on a long and crooked journey of constant learning.'

Number 14 baffled Yellowstone's professional staff more than most, and appears to have got under the skin of Doug Smith. The summer after her death, he rode out on horseback 'to find what was left of her. Not surprisingly, little was waiting for me but bone and hide. I found too the dead moose she'd been battling with, also entirely consumed by scavengers. I knelt one last time by her tattered carcase, feeling the quiet of this extraordinary spot in the Yellowstone back-country. A slight breeze came up, fingering the tall summer grass. Looking around, all in all it seemed a beautiful place to come to rest.'

The entire Yellowstone reintroduction project was only possible because of the Nez Perce tribe and its particular relationship with wolves. The first wolves were released onto the Nez Perce reservation; the tribe offered them a home at a time when state authorities refused to handle wolf management programmes. Wolf reintroduction was political dynamite, and politics prevailed over wolves. Only eighty years before, the US government initiated a policy of wolf extermination, a state of affairs that lasted until 1973 when President Richard Nixon signed the Endangered Species Act. The wolf was the first animal to be listed as endangered.

Few people would have blamed the Nez Perces if they had declined to assist the United States government in the resettlement of Canadian wolves into

Yellowstone. Historically, no tribe was treated more brutally by white America than the Nez Perces, but as the head of the recovery programme Ed Bangs put it, 'The Nez Perces revere wolves: they have a different way of looking at animals.'

Catherine Feher-Elston, an archaeologist and historian who has worked with many indigenous peoples across the world, wrote of the Nez Perce relationship with wolves in her 2004 book *Wolfsong*:

> Nez Perce call wolf He'me. Wolf is an embodiment of past, present and future to them . . . Levi Holt, a Nez Perce who worked with the wolves, maintains that wolf recovery helps return the Nez Perces and all people to balance, dignity and the right way to live. 'Restoring the wolf, protecting the wolf, sharing our lives with the wolf gives us a chance to have our culture reborn,' says Holt. 'We know that successful recovery will lead to delisting of the wolf. We know that some ranchers fear wolves will hurt their livestock. We know that if states take over wolf management and wolves are delisted, some people will hunt wolves. But our tribe will not take part in hunting wolves. People will not be allowed to hunt them on Nez Perce lands. We will honour our ancient relationships. What affects them affects us.'

> Holt says that when he remembers everything the wolves and his own tribe have endured together, he looks at the wolves and prays, 'We mourned your death. We were saddened by your exile. We rejoice in your return.'

The Last Wolf

Remember these things whenever you encounter stories of the wolf's savagery, stories of the wolf as a wilful slaughterer of innocent children, a terroriser of isolated human communities, a despoiler of human graves, a devourer of battlefield corpses; whenever you encounter the wolf cast in the Devil's clothes, remember too that where people have always lived closely with wolves and still do, they are often protective of the relationship and sometimes pray for them.

CHAPTER 2

A Cold Spoor

Was Waternish perhaps the last hold of heathendom in Skye, as it certainly was of wolves?

– Otta Swire, *Skye – The Island and Its Legends* (1961)

SOMETIMES YOU just have to walk the landscape to see what rubs off. You go with no more than half an idea in your head: something happened here once, you tell yourself, or someone else has told you and you at least half-believe it. And you want to know if the landscape itself still holds the scent or the sense of it. It is a nature writer's way of looking at the landscape. You go with your senses open to anything and everything, looking for the cold spoor of what it was that passed this way. Even a cold spoor is better than no spoor at all. Perhaps there will be a whiff of something on the wind. Perhaps the long absence of wolves will drop hints of their old presence the way something suggestive of what unfurled and died and vanished there forever seems to occur when you walk the battlefield of Culloden. When the naturalist and nature writer David Stephen wrote a novel about Scotland's last wolf he called the wolf Alba, the Gaelic word for Scotland. His was a symbolic wolf that died on 16 April 1746, the date of Culloden. Scotland died, he was saying, with Culloden, the last battle fought on British soil, and the wolf died with it. It is certainly unarguable that both events impoverished Scotland immeasurably.

Yet Culloden is a known historical event with a known outcome. There were eyewitnesses and survivors. As a species, we write down our own story. But in the matter of Scotland's wolves, there are almost no certainties at all. The more I explored our old wolf stories, the more elusive the truth became. The few historical accounts of wolf-related events are rich in distortion and quite bereft of what we now know in the twenty-first century about wolf biology. Yet the wolf has not changed. The wolf the Yellowstone Wolf Project began to reintroduce in 1995 (the project proceeds apace as I write) is the same wolf that storytellers from the Middle Ages to the Victorians crossed swords with, the same wolf that appears in the lens of a Norwegian wildlife cameraman in the twenty-first century. Yet it has become clear to me in the course of writing this book that almost nothing in so-called historical records about the wolf in Scotland is reliable, almost nothing at all.

So part of my response has been to walk the landscape to see what rubs off. Perhaps the old rocks, the oldest trees will speak to me more directly and with more honesty than the ghosts of the old people. So I travel, hoping against hope that perhaps just being there will flush out some extra awareness that lives on in that landscape, a connection that illuminates the past and makes it relevant to what the poet Kathleen

Raine called 'this very here and now of clouds moving across a still sky'.

I began with the north-leaning peninsula of Waternish on the island of Skye in search of the scent or the sense of its wolves. The particular half-an-idea that directed my feet there had been implanted by Seton Gordon, an old sage of both Skye and nature writing. His long life (he died in 1977 at the age of 90) and his fascination for both wildlife and the handed-down word-of-mouth history of the landscape and its people gave him a reach far back beyond the range of most writers of his time. And he had written in *The Charm of Skye* (1928) about wolf pits on a Waternish hillside. And Skye has a place in my heart not easily explained considering I am an east-coast mainlander from Dundee, and the slightest excuse to return has always been fine with me.

Waternish, or Vaternish in the old maps and old books like Seton Gordon's, is out-on-a-limb Skye. Skye is the Winged Isle of the Norseman. Of the island's four 'wings', Sleat boasts two ferry terminals and one end of the Skye Bridge, Duirinish is veined enough with roads for a stranger to need a road map, and Trotternish has a ferry connection to the Western Isles, a ring road, a couple of hairy east-west road crossings and Portree on the doorstep. But Waternish owns only a thin string of road that runs between the crest of a long hill and the sea. It begins with Fairy Bridge and ends with Trumpan, the one a by-passed stone bridge with a reputation for supernatural encounters and spooking horses, the other a ruined church famed for a massacre, and for the last resting place of a notorious madwoman. And nearby is

Cnoc a' Chrochaidh, the Hanging Knoll. There is little here to mitigate Waternish's isolation.

There is also something almost tangibly Norse at work, something more redolent of Shetland than Skye. There is a clutch of Norse-tongued names – Lustra, Halistra, Dun Hallin, Trumpan, the offshore islands of Isay, Mingay and Clett. And Waternish feels like its own island with a land bridge to Skye, much like Ardnamurchan's barely physical attachment to mainland Scotland, and which makes for self-containment in a community. Some islanders elsewhere on Skye look askance at the Waternish folk, and doubtless vice versa. The landscape of Waternish is a factor in all this too, for in terms of its blunt, raw beauty, and especially its seaward prospects, there is nothing like it, even on Skye.

Legend and historical fact (separating the two was never an easy task, especially among Gaels) have conspired to blacken the reputation of Waternish. Every legend is liberally bloodied, witches performed black deeds in the guise of cats, the centuries-old MacLeod-MacDonald feud commemorated at Trumpan was gruesome even by their own dire standards of clan warfare, and – wouldn't you believe it? – the peninsula has the reputation of being Skye's stronghold of wolves. Whether this last claim accounts for much of the darker side of Waternish lore is nothing more than speculation of my own, but I now advance it with some confidence because it is true of almost all the reputed haunts of wolves throughout Scotland. For all the cultural sophistication of the Gaels, they suffered from the same blind prejudice towards the wolf as most other northern European peoples, the same willingness to blacken its reputation at every opportunity. That the Gaels willingly exterminated wolves from their realm makes them no more and no less culpable than most of the rest of Scots, Britons, and half the tribes of the northern hemisphere. If wolves or stories of wolves have a home on Skye, here is as likely as anywhere and likelier than most.

But Waternish was still early in my explorations of the landscape of Scotland's wolves. It seems to me now that if there ever were wolves on Skye (and hints of a tradition prove nothing, not in the flaky depths of that malaise of Scotland's wolf landscape I think of as 'last wolf syndrome', a previously undiscovered chronic medical condition that attacks the corner of the human brain dealing in rational thought), it might have been in just such a far-flung northern outpost that they clung on longest, that they made their last stand in the face of the relentless encroachment and wolf-hatred of the people. The coastal woods under Geary and the tumultuous alders at Waternish House suggest that, three or four hundred years ago, Waternish would have been more wooded than it is now, and that too could have assisted their tenuous survival, although woodland has never been essential to wolves. Seton Gordon had written:

> Other relics of the past age are the remains of long wolf traps. These are on the hill near Trumpan and must be of great age, for the oldest inhabitant has no tradition of when the last wolf was trapped in Skye. The traps are long pits dug into the hillside.

In length they are some 24 feet, and in breadth approximately three feet. They are now almost filled in, but their shape can be seen at a glance. The entrance, too, is visible. There is a tradition among the old people of Waternish that the bait for the wolves was a piece of flesh placed near the upper end of the trap – the traps were all dug parallel with the slope of the hill – and presumably the wolf was imprisoned on entering by a door which closed behind it.

Here was my first brush with contradiction in the matter of communities and their wolf traditions. The 'oldest inhabitant' had no tradition of when the last wolf was trapped, yet the 'old people' did have a tradition about how the trap was made and baited. And then there was the truly implausible bit, as recorded by Otta Swire in her book, *Skye – The Island and Its Legends* (1961):

There are still faint traces of ancient wolf-traps to be seen. Indeed, so comparatively recent are they that tradition still lingers of how a hunter accidentally fell into his trap and was saved by his companion, one Gillie Chriosd Chaim, who caught the wolf by the tail and so held it . . .

Um. Typical wolf behaviour might have been either to back away from the man who had fallen in, or to scramble free itself (and if a man could do it, rest assured a wolf could do it with ease). The one element of the story likely to have induced a hostile reaction in the wolf is the Alice-in-Wonderland-ish detail of someone else coming up behind it and grabbing its tail, an idea about as likely in the real world as the Mad Hatter's tea party. It is a shame that the wolf declines in real life to live up to its ancient reputation, for there would have been a delicious natural justice if the hunter had been torn apart in his own pit by the very quarry whose death the pit had been designed to achieve.

Elsewhere on Skye, at Prince Charlie's Cave near Elgol, Otta Swire notes that it has a claim to be where 'one of the earlier Mackinnon chiefs, being attacked by a wolf, slew the creature by forcing a deer bone down its throat, a feat still commemorated in the Mackinnon arms.'

Despite the Grimm-esque quality of the yarn-spinning, she is confident enough to assess Waternish's reputation thus: 'Was it perhaps the last hold of heathendom in Skye, as it certainly was of wolves?' Yet no-one has ever supplied a scrap of evidence to back up that 'certainly'.

Back in the real world of Waternish in December, I looked out across Loch Bay where a conifer plantation ends and the cliff belt about the waist of Sgurr a Bhagh begins. Beneath it hang folds of skirts fashioned from native trees, untrampled, ungrazed, unfelled, unburned, the natural order. I watched them grow grey and darkly purple one quiet midwinter afternoon and thought the wolves would have loved them.

There were only two hours of usable daylight left. There was no prospect of afterglow or moonlight to steal from the long northern night, merely the certainty of a dirty afternoon, a week before the shortest day, growing progressively dirtier. Wind had blasted rain into submission, but that was all that had submitted. It had looked an unenticing prospect when the squalls thudded through a half-dark noon, but by one o'clock they had ceased their percussive flaying of the window where I worked, and I rose from the writing table and went out into the island. By two I was scrambling through a little gully on the flank of Beinn na Boineide and the air was the icy breath of the Arctic. If anything else was to fall from that sky that day it would be snow.

I have long since learned to value fragments stolen from the unlikeliest days: two hours on a hillside in Waternish can amount to an energising expedition after a long morning writing. A mind weary with word-making can be blown clean and uncluttered, and goes eagerly in pursuit of the wolf image it has made for itself. There is no long, patient stalk to consider, nothing to pack, nothing to prepare. There is just jacket, scarf, wellies, gloves, binoculars and an afterthought apple for my pocket. Then there is just the being there.

I love the gloaming hour whatever the season, the folding away of the daylight creatures and the unfolding of night lives, the brief pause of overlapping regimes. Here an owl might contemplate an eagle, the turning head of a wind-perched kestrel might follow a low-flying skein of whooper swans homing in on a roosting lochan. At the same hour on a December day a decade or two before Culloden, a fox might have stepped deferentially aside from a hunting wolf.

At a little over 1,000 feet, Beinn na Boineide, the Bonnet Hill, is the head and shoulders of all Water-nish. I tramped up out of the gully, breathed easier on the slopes above, saw the sea widen and Waternish's own shape and shade of moorland hill lengthen. With no light in the sky the moor grasses smouldered with their own dark flame. There was no bright point in all the landscape. A slab of dark grey cloud lowered and squatted on Waternish, so I walked north keeping below it, following the line of overgrown dykes until I stumbled on the bed of an old track. A slow, downhill, breaking wave of peat and moss and lichen had overwhelmed the bones of dykes and track, obliterated the art of the builders. If there was anything left of the old wolf traps, if I could find what was left, if there had ever been wolf traps at all other than in a storyteller's imagination, this was what I could expect to find . . . their grown-over ghosts.

Once I would have walked here among birch, hazel, oak, ash, rowan, alder, willow, pine, aspen maybe, an airy woodland shaped into contrary uphill waves by the sea wind. Once, the road-and-dyke builder might have stood here among such trees and watched a wolf catch his scent on the wind, test it, and step quietly away from it. I allowed myself to believe that much, for the moment. Then a buzzard cried close by and almost at once rounded a buttress moving sideways across the strengthening wind, led by the primary feathers of her left wing. And I was above and behind the bird, so I crouched to be a rock on the hillside, well placed to watch her harness the wind to her bidding. When I put the glasses on her she almost filled them.

She sat on the wind rather than hovering like a kestrel. She held her wings in rigid concave arches, flexing them only briefly to make minute adjustments of her position or to drift away a yard or two over the moor only to turn again into the wind, yellow legs dangling. Her head restlessly scanned the moor below, ahead and to either side, and to the far horizons. In perhaps ten minutes, she was never further than 20 yards from where I had first seen her. Then she started to drift towards me, sideways and slightly backwards, conceding a few yards of airspace to the wind. As the bird drifted, she also rose, climbing the hillside backwards. In that attitude she passed above my head, low and dark and huge. Instantly the tables were turned. Now she was above and behind me, and I guessed that her scrutiny of the landscape was now riveted on me: the watcher watched.

Or the hunter hunted. So I thought, of course, of the hunter who fell into the wolf pit. And when the buzzard called again, she was so close that I wondered if she might take my moor-coloured stillness at face value, mistake my hooded, hunched shape for a rock, and make a taloned perch of me. But it was only the steely downcurving edge of her voice that cleaved through me and put an iced chill between my shoulder blades. I felt something between primitive thrill and cold electric shock, neither of them particularly comfortable.

I reasoned then that perhaps she was merely assessing my unfamiliar shape in her territory where every rock and parcel of bog was a know landmark. I would play the rock a little longer and see what unfolded.

Absence of movement sharpens the senses. I became intensely aware of everything I could see without moving. A tiny lizard, looking ancient, flickered over a bare patch among the heather; a black and grey boat emerged from a hidden shore; a grey horse kicked the air on a croft and a kestrel crossed its field, fast and downwind; the boat pirouetted in a bay and stopped; a vivid orange spider the size of a small button crossed the lizard's patch of bare earth.

Where was the buzzard?

I tried listening for her, but the wind was a thudding wail now and nothing else carried through. I began to move my head, slowly, left and right, searching as much of the land and sky as came into my view. Nothing. But that still left all of Waternish above and behind me at the bird's disposal. I pushed my head as far back as I could to stare up at the sky above me, the empty sky above me. But I sensed she was still there. Finally, I conceded defeat to the freezing pounding of the wind. I stood slowly and stiffly, and turned. She was about a dozen yards away, regarding me side-headed with one orange eye. She hung there a moment longer, then a shimmy and a dipped wing and a raising and lowering of her legs took her to a new stance on the wind below and ahead of me again. She had enough confidence in her place on that hillside to turn her back on me and go about her business, having established to her satisfaction that I had no part to play in it.

She then revealed just what her business was. She abandoned her airy perch, thrust forward her legs, threw high both wings and landed 20 yards away, dipped her head into a small, hidden hollow, and when she raised it again to look up at me it was bloodied. All was prosaically explained. I had put the bird up from a sheep carcase when she first drew herself to my attention. She had lingered to see if I posed a threat to her meal. Having decided I did not have what it takes to sunder rotting sheep flesh, she returned to her meal, still watching.

I backed off to a higher rock where I could watch and leave her in peace. The new viewpoint revealed the carcase – not sheep, though, but fox. Whatever had killed the fox in the first place, it was not the buzzard; eagle, perhaps, or gamekeeper.

The Minch was wide and wan and eerie green, and a tightly-marshalled flotilla of showers was about to flay the shore up at Trumpan. I walked north to meet them, and to look for wolf pits, and as I walked I thought about the buzzard and how it had responded to my sudden arrival calmly and without a single threatening gesture. Just like a wolf, I thought, so confident of her place in her territory.

So I came in low light to the hillside above Trumpan. Bearing in mind that Seton Gordon had said that the wolf traps were 'now almost filled in, but their shape can be seen at a glance', and bearing in mind that was 80 or 90 years ago and finding anything would be the most outrageous fluke, I then stumbled across an out-rageous fluke. There was . . . something . . . on the hillside, a faint depression, a rectangle that ran parallel to the slope of the hill as he had described but both shorter and wider than his measurements, and looking in all honesty like nothing at all. And if I had gone there without reading Seton Gordon's book I would not have given it a second glance, or even a first one . . . except that there was another, fainter but similar depression nearby.

It was all but dark by now, and I needed the last of the light to get down to the road so that I could walk back to my temporary accommodation without getting lost. Besides, there seemed no point in lingering. There was nothing to look at other than two more or less discernible rectangles on the surface of the moor, and these could have been anything or nothing, or, tottering on the edge of improbability, they could have been wolf traps four hundred years ago.

I would go back some time later to look at them in good light. I would scour that same patch of hillside for an hour and I would find nothing at all, no hint that they had ever been. And such is the elusive nature of the wolf in the pages of our history; such is the elusive nature of the wolf wherever he still lives on the face of the earth, sometimes a shadow moving at the edge of things, sometimes nothing at all.

CHAPTER 3
An Unreliable History

In the Navajo Way, people are responsible for taking good care of their livestock. If a wolf takes a sheep, it is not the fault of the wolf. The wolf is only behaving like a wolf. The shepherd is the guilty one – for not paying close attention and protecting the flock.

– Catherine Feher-Elson, *Wolf Song*, 2004

THERE CAN BE no reliable history of the wolf. Histories, after all, are only ever written by people, and there is no species less qualified and less entitled than yours and mine to write that particular history. Our relationship with the wolf has lurched between reverence and revulsion depending on time and geography and religion and a few other variables and human failings less easy to pin down, and it is shot through with the most profound misunderstanding and questionable behaviour. For example: when the Pleistocene was in its pomp, sometime between 1.8 million and 10,000 years ago, and the wolf was the most widespread mammal in the northern hemisphere, it also became the first mammal we ever domesticated, long before we were tempted by either cattle or horses. That fact alone must mean that the wolf had qualities that impressed those distant ancestors. You don't invite a monster into your home. All our dogs are descended from that one source, fashioned to our specific needs by selective breeding, so 'all our dogs' must include the wolfhounds we eventually learned to breed specifically to kill wolves.

What happened? How did we progress from a relationship with wolves that had admiration at its core to one in which we have marshalled all the forces of human ingenuity to indulge an unslakeable thirst for killing wolves? That obsession's most gruesome manifestation is also the most recent – shooting them from aircraft. So what follows must be an unreliable history, which is the only kind I am qualified to write.

People have exaggerated everything about wolves forever, but especially their size. The presumption is that they are hefty and huge, and they are neither. The average weight of a mature European wolf is around 85lbs, slightly more than in North America. The largest animals will weigh over 100lbs, but very rarely over 120. (One famous Alaskan wolf killed in 1939 weighed 175lbs, but that was a creature rarer than a seven-foot-tall human. Nevertheless, many people who read that single statistic will tell you for the rest of their lives that wolves weigh 175lbs, and I have met others who will round it up to 200lbs if only because it confirms our age-old misconception.) The average size from nose to tip of tail is around five-and-a-half feet, occasionally as long as six feet, the height at the shoulder around 30 inches. Most people's reaction to their first sight of a wolf is that it is smaller than they imagined, its legs are longer, and its feet are huge. First responses almost never mention teeth.

The grey wolf, *canis lupus*, evolved out of sundry North American ancestors early in the Pleistocene, and established itself in Russia and Northern Europe by way of a land bridge left high and dry by falling sea levels where the Bering Strait now separates Alaska and Siberia. That land bridge was fundamental to the wolf's story, for it evolved into rich grassland, and it tempted some of the teeming, wandering herds of the North American plains and forests to travel into the vast Eurasian landmass beyond. Among other things, Eurasia acquired the horse that way.

Predators followed the herds, especially a great traveller like the wolf. This spectacular era of plenty prompted the wolf to expand its ambitions and its horizons, colonising the Arctic fringes, mountains, and even deserts as it travelled. But eras of plenty are notoriously finite, and that one ended with a prolonged climate upheaval we now call the Wisconsin period, 8,000 years of colossal natural turmoil. Many species vanished from the earth, and incredible as it sounds now, the horse vanished from North America, although because it had crossed the land bridge into Europe, it could – and did – eventually wander back again by the same route.

The Wisconsin period ended with the end of the last ice age, and two species in particular emerged from it in positions of strength by virtue of their adaptability and resourcefulness. *Canis lupus* was one, and *Homo sapiens* was the other. When the one had first become aware of the other, both species were hunters, and the wolf was rather better at it. Wherever in the world a thoughtful relationship between man and wolf still remains, there is ample evidence – carved, painted, written and word-of-mouth – of an ancient and inherited respect for the wolf as a teacher. It is one of the great ironies of the evolution of our species that long before we began to think in terms of exterminating the wolf we spent a great many centuries learning to be more wolf-like, learning not just how to hunt more efficiently but also how to live better lives, by inclining towards a society based on the family unit that was both independent and interdependent, but also permitted the wanderers, the loners, the ones that never quite fitted in with the family structure. Today we are still apt to refer to such people as 'a bit of a lone wolf', and that may be truer than we think; it may be all that has survived from that ancient era when our forefathers watched the wolf and saw a role model there.

The change began when we started to consider the possibilities of a settled rather than a nomadic existence. The moment that we thought of harnessing sheep, cattle and horses to do our bidding was surely preceded by the moment we realised we could shape the world around us at our bidding too. Perhaps it began when someone saw a great tree felled by a storm, and began to wonder how to fell many trees. Perhaps it was lightning that felled the great tree and someone began to wonder how to make lightning to fell trees, and stumbled on the notion of using fire as a tool. With fire at his disposal, man learned that he could make meadows where he wanted them to be rather than where he came across them, and instead of wandering from place to place, he could corral his animals into one place, and that would be the place where he lived.

And that was the place where the wolf he had so long admired became his sworn enemy, because in the eyes of the wolf a gathering of animals in one place was where it hunted, and in the eyes of the man, the gathering of animals in one place had suddenly become his livelihood and the wolf had suddenly become a threat to it.

The changed relationship did not happen everywhere and it did not happen all at once, but it seeped like a slow tide through Europe and Russia, and in time it would be carried by white settlers to the New World. By then, of course, religion in general and Christianity in particular had transformed our ideas about our relationship with the natural world. Suddenly a jealous God had given us dominion over all the other creatures. Suddenly the Son of God was the Good Shepherd who gave his life for the flock, and everyone knew that the flock's number one enemy was the wolf. So if Christ was the Good Shepherd, the wolf was demonised as the agent of the Devil. An illustration in the *Book of Kells* shows a wolf with the Devil's tail instead of a wolf tail, a character assassination worthy of Gerald Scarfe. Christianity has always made exceptions in its doctrine of compassion and turning the other cheek.

The further back you go, you find religious ideas that were deeper and deeper embedded in the natural world. The very seasons of the year were marked by rituals. The harvest thanksgiving is perhaps the oldest religious idea in the mind of settled man. All that has changed is the recipient of the thanks. But it was the notion of a 'spirit' that marked the beginnings of his religious journeys, and that was one he extended to the animals. In the earliest hunting cultures, man felt the need to appease the spirit world. Deer, elk, reindeer, buffalo, bison, beaver, bear, boar, salmon . . . whatever the quarry, they all had spirits, and the hunter implored them for a kind of forgiveness before he hunted. The most potent spirits like raven, eagle, wolf, whale, had a power to influence the lives of people we can only guess at now, but you find echoes of them in the literature and the folklore of, for example, the Native American tribes, Inuit people from Alaska to the Canadian Arctic and Greenland, and many European races from the reindeer-herding Laplanders in the north to the ancient Greeks in the south. However and wherever and whatever you hunted, when you hunted for a living you worked with a mindset that was common to much of the northern hemisphere of the world. You invoked the protection of the spirits of the animal world and you employed animal cunning, animal techniques, animal strategies, for you were animal yourself and you saw some animals as your equal. But you saw the wolf as a teacher.

You hunted wolves too, not to eat them but to wear them. I met a man in Alaska who ran a dog-sled business. He showed me the parkas and mitts he wore and provided for his clients. The hood trim and the mitts were wolf skin. I asked why that was necessary, given that there were so many man-made alternatives today. Yes, he agreed, and as one who admired wolves he had tried them all.

'But nothing else gets close to wolf skin,' he said. 'It's why wolves wear it.'

He said he had never yet met a new client who was indifferent to the fact that they had just learned they would be wearing wolf skin on their sled-dog trips.

'Many of them are hunters and already have their own, but if they don't they mostly leave here swearing they're going to buy it. And it's not just about the overwhelming efficiency of wolf skin as a material. They appear to feel something else, a connection. They don't all own up to it, and those that do can't always articulate it, and it always takes them by surprise.'

What they are giving voice to is something very, very old. Hunters in many ancient northern cultures disguised themselves in wolf skins, sometimes a complete skin, sometimes a cape with the wolf head for a hood, and they believed they borrowed from the wolf when they wore it. It is a short step from that to the elevated mythological status of the wolf in countless rituals of fertility and death, and another short step from that to the place of the wolf in the hierarchy of the Gods (Apollo's mother appeared as a wolf, Odin's reign was ended by a wolf), and from that to the idea of the hunter who parts with his soul in exchange for extraordinary powers, wolf-like powers for example.

That way lies the extreme perversion of werewolves that haunted Europe in the Middle Ages, a cult that believed that a sacrificed human would wander the world as a wild beast. The lone wolf had become something very sinister indeed.

Nothing captures the spirit of that era more succinctly than the story of Red Riding Hood, surely the world's most famous blackening of the wolf's character, a story that has probably never been out of print since it was first written down in France in the late seventeenth century, but which is much older than that. The hooded cape was a symbol of witchcraft, and wolf-worship sects were just one more unhealthy product of the age. Red Riding Hood's origins may lie in a conflict between two occult sects that didn't get on, one male and one female. The story lives on as a salutary warning to children not to engage with strangers, but draws no moral from the idea that the child is incapable of telling the difference between her grandmother and a wolf wearing a bonnet. I blame the parents. But then logic has never played a very prominent part in our relationship with the wolf.

As a Scottish nature writer living and working in my native land, I am surrounded by landscapes that are famed around the world for their beauty, but which are, nevertheless, impoverished by the fact that they have been wolf-less for at least 200 years. I am surrounded too by the fall-out from 2,000 demonising years – dense and all-but-impenetrable thickets of superstition, ignorance, accidental and deliberate disinformation and downright lies, all of it designed to keep the wolf where it belongs – in other people's countries. The unreliable history of wolves is nowhere more unreliable than on my own doorstep.

At the heart of it is the idea much promulgated in several centuries of literature that Scotland was a place made fearful by impassable forests populated by all manner of ferocious creatures so that the few travellers moved through the country in fear of their lives. And what they feared most, of course, was the wolf. Those early writers would have us believe that the forests were overrun with wolves.

Shelters called spittals were built here and there in the Highlands as refuges for travellers. One historic source suggests apertures were let into the walls so that the traveller could spy the land for wolves. They were called loup-holes and from them the language acquired a new word, loophole, a means of evasion. That part at least could be true. The rest is a grotesque blanket of gross exaggeration draped over a handful of grains of truth.

Yes, there were some extensive natural forests, but Scotland never grew 'impassable' forests. The Scots pine was the dominant tree in most of those forests, and by its very nature it creates spacious forests. Yes, there were wolves, and certainly until Christianity became widespread perhaps a thousand years ago and medieval kings established hunting parks in both Scotland and England, conditions were more or less perfect for them. There were many red deer, and these are forest animals at heart and were only banished to the open hills by the Victorians. The forest red deer is perhaps a third larger than the animals we see on bare Highland hills today, and it was the preferred prey species of Scotland's wolves, and if we reintroduced the wolf today it still would be. There were moose and reindeer too, and wild goats and wild boar. There were more predators too, including lynx and the European brown bear. And the people, of course, constantly refining their weapons and their hunting strategies, as they do to this day.

Until the industrial revolution, much of Scotland's human population lived on the land. Wealth was reckoned in cattle which they moved through the hills to the markets in the south, and which one clan routinely stole from another and hid in quiet corries, and that too was very much to the wolf's liking. So yes, the people suffered from the presence of the wolves, and 'the wolf at the door' was not a threat to the people inside the door but to their herds outside it, and therefore to the economic survival of the people. And so yes, there would have been a time when more or less every available wolf territory was occupied and the howl of the wolf was a familiar anthem to the native humans. People who live with wolves now, and who are descended from unbroken millennia of people who lived and evolved with wolves, will tell you of the power of that sound, especially when you cannot see the wolves that are howling (for the howl of a wolf can travel five miles in still weather). Perhaps that is the root of the terror in the breast of Highland travellers in the days of wolf plenty: it was not that they were physically terrorised by the wolves themselves, but rather what their imagination did with the raised voices of a wolf pack they never saw, quite possibly because it was five miles away. They would not know – and they would not believe if they were told – that wolves hunt in silence, that howling is nothing more sinister than wolf-to-wolf communication.

The medieval period seemed to have been something of a watershed in the fortunes of the wolf. In Scotland and in England, kings formalised their love of hunting by creating royal parks inside endless miles of fencing. Predators were eliminated inside the parks, and deer stocks decimated by over-hunting were topped up from elsewhere in the realm, and within a few generations the native deer stock was almost obliterated. Yet there remained a stubborn Europe-wide belief among hunting kings that if they killed off the wolves the deer stocks would increase. Yes, but only if they learned to moderate their hunting habits, which they never did.

Edward I of England took that philosophy to its illogical conclusion when in 1281 he commissioned hunters to eliminate the wolf from the land. His project was so ruthless and so efficient that the wolf was gone within a decade. Without the perceived threat of the wolf in the wild places of England, hunting burgeoned as never before, and soon the roe deer was extinct.

From that day to this, land managers driven by self-interest and oblivious to the self-evident truths of conservation and bio-diversity have knee-jerked their way from one quick fix to the next. In nineteenth-century Scandinavia, farmers decided to try and eliminate the elk so that there was less competition for their own grazing herds of cattle and sheep. But the elk was the wolf's main prey species, and in its absence they turned to the next best thing – the very sheep and cattle the farmers wanted to have all the grass. Thousands of peasants were dragooned into an almost military operation to kill the wolves. So a chain reaction began, and within a generation it had wrecked an ecosystem that had evolved for millennia. In time, of course, they had to reintroduce the elk and the wolf simply walked back when no-one was looking. In the twenty-first century, elk-hunters and sheep farmers want to drive out the wolf from parts of Scandanavia again.

And in the Abruzzi mountains in Italy in the 1970s, wolf biologist Erik Zimen found that wolves were feeding off mountain villagers' refuse at night. When he investigated the problem he discovered that the local deer population had been exterminated by hunters, so he initiated a deer reintroduction programme and the wolves reverted to type and vanished from the village streets. He had simply put back a missing link in the chain. But it seems the lesson still has to be learned again and again.

And yet, and yet, even throughout the many centuries of wolf persecution, even as they were being hunted to extinction in many regions of America and Europe, a passionate reverence for wolves has co-existed alongside the loathing, almost exclusively among human enclaves where the relationship with wolves is ancient and unbroken. From the Indians of the great plains to the Inuit of northmost America and Canada to the Laplanders of northmost Europe to the mountain villages of Mediterranean lands, wolves never lost their revered status at the heart of tribal society. They were invoked in rituals of death, fertility, and hunting, admired for their strength, resilience, hunting skills, the social cohesion of the pack, the determined independence of the lone wolf. Nomadic tribes saw themselves in the wolves' endurance as tireless travellers. Inevitably, such an intimate relationship between man and beast produced extraordinary legend-making, none of it more extraordinary than the phenomenon of 'wolf children'. It is biologically impossible for wolves to suckle children, but the imagery is created out of a view of the wolf as a wholly benevolent presence.

There is no more celebrated piece of pro-wolf propaganda in history than the story of Romulus and

Remus. It was widespread 2,000 years ago throughout Mediterranean Europe, and the possibility that it originated many centuries earlier on Crete rather than in Italy has done nothing to inhibit its durability or its fame as the founding myth of the Italian nation. Romulus and Remus were twin brothers, the fruit of an unlikely union between Mars, who was the Roman god of war, and a princess variously called Ilia, Rhea, Silvia or Rhea Silvia. Mars, being a god with a 24/7 lifestyle, seems to have abandoned his mistress to the role of single parent. This state of affairs left her vulnerable to the evil intentions of her uncle Amulius, who had the twins banished to the wilderness where he was confident they would die a pitiable death. Unluckily for him, but luckily for legend-making, they sheltered in a cave where they were found by a she-wolf, who suckled them and kept them alive, until a peasant called Faustulus stumbled across them and took them home. He and his wife Acca Larenia raised them as their own children. They obviously had enlightened parenting skills, for Romulus went on to found the city of Rome, which he modestly named after himself, in the suspiciously precise year of 753 BC.

Somewhere along the way the twins fell out. Whatever the source of the dispute, Romulus killed his brother. Perhaps Remus wanted Roma to be called Rema, who knows? But by then the twins' fame and their apparent powers of persuasion had achieved reconciliation between the Romans and the neighbouring warmongering Sabines. The twins had become symbolic of the union of the two races within Rome's embrace, and at a stroke the wolf became the emblematic figurehead of the Roman Empire: it had, after all, nurtured the founder of Rome, and it had long been an object of worship in the Sabines' animist religion.

The survival of some tattered remnants of traditions born in the heyday of the Sabines may still explain the tolerance shown to the wolf even today along Europe's Mediterranean edge. But in the far north of Europe, human attitudes towards the wolf – and particularly those of the Laplanders – are shaped by the inevitable ambivalence that characterises a race of reindeer herders who were also historically hunters. The Lapps, or Sammi, had developed a technique of chasing down wolves with broad skis on deep new snow across the open *fjeld*, and those who did not own guns had developed ski-sticks with a stabbing point, two more examples of the man's ingenuity in his endless war on wolves. Erik Zimen's 1981 book *The Wolf* reveals some of the consequences in cold statistics:

> In winter domestic animals were kept securely indoors and, as the numbers of natural prey animals had been greatly reduced, the wolves suffered from acute food shortage. This, combined with the enormous pressure put on them by hunting, resulted in a drastic reduction in their numbers within a few years. Between 1827 and 1839 about 500 wolves a year were killed in Sweden, but 20 years later, in 1860, the figure was only 100. A similar drastic reduction took place in Norway and Finland between ten and twenty years later . . . The wolf was restricted to his last refuge areas in the wide, treeless, mountainous areas of the northwest

. . . and found security in these almost uninhabited and inaccessible regions, and, thanks to the reindeer, plenty of food. But the Laplanders' campaign against him continued.

I wonder about those numbers. As we will see, the nineteenth century was probably the nadir of the relationship between man and wolf, its propaganda the vilest, its contribution to wolf history the most unreliable. It is all too easy to look at something 150 years old and treat it as wise simply because it is old. I have learned to treat every statistic I have seen about wolves with outright hostility – guilty until proved innocent. Killing wolves at the rate of 500 a year in a country the size of Sweden sounds like an overestimate of around 450. It's so easy to slip an extra zero into the figures over 150 years. But the point is made: the wolf was systematically driven out of all but the wildest landscapes. New roads, aircraft, and the snowmobile with what Zimen called 'its ecologically devastating effects' took new tolls even in deepest wilderness.

The Swedish nature conservation office conducted an inquiry into the distribution and numbers of the four big predators – the wolf, the lynx, the wolverine and the bear – between 1960–64. They found that the wolf was gravely endangered. The few survivors travelled great distances, no doubt an adaptation to the perpetual hunting. The result of the inquiry was public debate on whether the wolf should be protected. Surprisingly enough, many Laplanders came out on the wolf's side.

In spite of the traditional hostility to the wolf, they must have felt respect and admiration for it.

But as long as there are wolves in reindeer areas, there are bound to be conflicts with the interest of the Laplanders, and revival of the wolf in this region therefore seems unlikely. Nevertheless, the increasingly understanding and tolerant attitude of the Laplanders towards their hereditary enemy gives some reason for hope.

Catherine Feher-Elston's *Wolf Song* found an unusual source that might explain the ancient foundation of that hope, an abundance of amber:

> The Sammi . . . maintain that there is a sacred connection between the glittering gold colour of wolf eyes and amber. The amber eyes of the wolf are linked to celestial events – comets, 'falling stars', and lightning. The full moon is a special ally of the wolf, and both moon and wolf are sacred to the Sammi . . . It is said that when wolves encounter amber, they make prayers to it and kiss the fossilized resin to gain strength and power and communicate with the sacred powers of the sky.

Such ideas do not sit well with contemporary science, but in a world driven by the global economy it never does any harm to be reminded that many human attitudes to nature were founded among isolated tribes, and that bonds forged with nature in isolation are infinitely more durable than global deals that recognise billions of dollars as their only yardstick. The invention of the snowmobile does not cancel out the historical truths that people are capable of extraordinary acts of faith, that in the countless eras of the Lapps' evolution before the snowmobile was invented, they lived their lives at nature's bidding, and they would find sacred things in the wolf as well as inconvenience to their reindeer-dependent economy.

Catherine Feher-Elston uncovered an even more surprising man-wolf relationship in her own country among the Navajo, one that the twenty-first-century European sheep farmer is not going to like one bit:

> In the Navajo Way, people are responsible for taking good care of their livestock. If a wolf takes a sheep, it is not the fault of the wolf. The wolf is only behaving like a wolf. The shepherd is the guilty one – for not paying close attention and protecting the flock. If too much predation occurs, a combination of negligence and disharmony must be the cause. A hatalii will be consulted to determine the cause of the problem. A ceremony or 'sing' will be held to bring the shepherd, flock and family back into harmony.

> All the clan relatives, friends and community will come to the sing to help restore balance. At the conclusion of the ceremonies, the land, people, animals and plants will benefit. Balance will be restored. All will walk again in Beauty.

We have grown so accustomed to the idea of the wolf as an adversary in so many parts of the northern hemisphere (and nowhere more so than in my own country, where we obliterated it more than 200 years ago) that the possibility of the wolf as a benevolent presence in our midst takes us aback. Yet it is every bit as widespread. And not all of it is rooted in the distant past. In 1998 I travelled to Alaska to make two radio programmes for the BBC, and there I met an independent wolf researcher called Gordon Haber. He was a man whose reputation had gone before him. He had studied with the great Adolph Murie, whose book *The Wolves of Mount McKinley* was one of a handful of seminal works that spawned the now flourishing literature that is American nature writing. Gordon Haber is comfortably the most uncompromising pro-wolf naturalist I have come across, and for many people uncomfortably the most uncompromising. But I like my champions of nature uncompromising. The good intentions of thousands of professional conservationists across the world are hamstrung by bureaucratic quests to 'achieve a balance' or to 'reconcile all the competing interests', a doomed philosophy that produces a political swamp and calls it wildness. Such people distrust the Gordon Habers of this world, distrust their certainty, their conviction, their single-minded belief that nature is a better manager of wild country than people, and in the particular case of Gordon Haber, that the wolf is the heartbeat of all of it. I liked him. I sensed a kindred spirit.

I came across his name again a few years later in a book called *The Company of Wolves* (1996) by Peter Steinhart, who was writing here about the changing nature of the relationship between man and wolf inside Alaska's Denali National Park (Denali is the old native name for Mount McKinley. and which has now been restored to both the mountain and the National Park):

> Gordon Haber reports that as more and more backpackers visit Denali, the wolves are becoming increasingly habituated to humans. 'It's an everyday event for wolves to walk up to people in the back country or campgrounds and sit down three feet from them,' says Haber. 'They pick up a book and walk off with it. They sniff a hand. People will say they looked over their shoulders and there was a wolf sniffing at their heels. It's a touching kind of relationship. The wolves are totally at ease. It's like "I see you as a friend."'

I love the implication that in the right circumstances, the man-wolf relationship may be reverting to its oldest prototype, in which curiosity begat friendship and mutual admiration. That way lies the salvation of the wild world. By and large the backpackers who trek into Denali National Park seek only the solace and sustenance of wilderness. This behaviour of wolves towards them is not necessarily untypical in places where the wolf population is strong and confident in its landscape and the people's presence is benevolent and unthreatening.

Haber must have found much to hearten him in a book called *Comeback Wolves – Western Writers Welcome the Wolf Home*. It is a collection of essays and poems edited by Gary Wockner, Gregory MacNamee and SueEllen Campbell and published in 2005 to celebrate the return of wolves to the American West. It draws its inspiration from one of those inexplicable lone-wolf journeys that punctuate our awareness of the way wolves behave and captivate the imagination of the wolf's admirers. The book is dedicated to Wolf 293 F, whose collared body was found on a highway near Idaho Springs, Colorado, where it had been hit by a truck. Its journey had begun in Yellowstone, 500 miles away. No-one knows why, and no-one ever will. But it offers the delicious temptation to believe that nature was sending an ambassador back across the Rockies into one of the wolf's historic strongholds (a stronghold from which it had been evicted by the white man) to see how the land lies now, to see what kind of welcome it might receive. The animal's prosaic death might have been the end of the affair, but the Yellowstone connection and the discovery of the heroic nature of the lone wolf's undertaking touched a nerve, and something very old and very primitive in the American West stirred into life. Many people there thought the wolf was long dead, but it turns out it was only hibernating. Whatever it was (and it might have been an echo of the pioneering spirit that emboldened the Founding Fathers and planted the seed of the American Dream) it touched hearts, and now the wolf is back in the West. This is from an essay in *Comeback Wolves* by Hal Clifford:

> But nature is saying . . . in the tracks of a lone wolf that came sniffing through Colorado not long ago, that I am here to be reckoned with on my own terms, and that you, Man, are part of me. You and I, we have a relationship.

We define and redefine the wolf, yet who owns the wolf? The question seems absurd, like asking who owns the wind or the river. Before the United States existed, the peoples who inhabited the American land didn't even recognize the idea of land ownership. The wolf existed on its own terms, for its own reasons, as all things did. That era has long gone, though, replaced by one in which we have not only private property rights (including the right to use the wind's power and the river's water), but also the Clean Air Act and Clean Water Act. And so the question must be asked and answered: All of us own the wolf, just as all of us own the air we breathe and the water we drink. We depend on air and water, of course. But we depend on the wolf, too, and we have a need to defend the wolf as we defend the air and water – for our own good, not simply for the wolf's.

. . . We are not wise enough to understand what in nature, if anything, is expendable. The less we understand (and we understand little), the more we must embrace the precautionary, quasi-religious strategy of proceeding with humility. We must keep all the parts. The act of doing so is our best insurance that nature – including us first and foremost – will thrive.

Beneath this practical argument lies a moral one: Nature is intrinsically valuable . . . We depend on life. All life depends on life.

Here and there in the world, a tide is turning back in favour of the wolf, in Yellowstone, Colorado, southern

Europe, Norway. In the wilderness of Alaska and Canada and parts of Russia its population remains buoyant enough to win new generations of admirers, and slowly those generations reared on the old dark stories are dying out. The modern chapters of the history are perhaps growing more reliable.

But now, what of my own country? Scotland, it seems to me, is a special case, and the only one with which I am truly in a position to take issue. After 21 years of making my living writing books and journalism about Scotland's wild landscapes and wildlife, of looking at nature in Scotland and thinking about what Scotland can do in favour of nature to redress a huge and longstanding imbalance, and after half a lifetime of scrutinising the evidence, it is clear to me that the wolf is at the heart of it all. One of our most durable difficulties, even as the second decade of the twenty-first century dawns, is the way that the wolf has been handed down to us, so that beliefs and fears are still held and still felt here many years after they have been shown up in more enlightened countries to be inventions of the Dark Ages. I have suggested that the nineteenth century was a low point in the unreliable history. I now suggest that Scotland was a landscape that promulgated hate-filled propaganda more zealously than any other. That combination – the Scottish landscape and the Victorian mindset – was truly awful. A handful of voices in particular compounded the countless felonies – Sir Walter Scott inevitably, one of his countless more-or-less-forgotten disciples called Sir Thomas Dick Lauder, two preposterous Jacobite brothers called Sobieski-Stuart, and the man who assembled their wacky outpourings and made them respectable in a single academic book, Professor J.E. Harting.

CHAPTER 4
The Rabid Droves

*It is related that William the Conqueror left
the dead bodies of the English upon the battlefield to be devoured by worms, wolves, birds
and dogs. When Waltheof, the son of Siward,
with an invading Danish army arrived in the
Humber in September 1069, and reinforced
by the men of Northumbria, made an attack
on York, it is related that 3,000 Normans fell.
A hundred of the chiefest rank were said to
have fallen amongst the flames by the hand of
Waltheof himself, and the Scalds of the North
sang how the son of Siward gave the corpses
of the Frenchmen as a choice banquet for the
Wolves of Northumberland.*

– J.E. Harting, *British Mammals Extinct
Within Historic Times* (1880)

PROFESSOR JAMES EDMUND HARTING, FLS.,
FZS, liked his bile undiluted when he dipped his pen in
it. The commonest word used by the Victorian generations to describe the presence of wolves in the landscape
is 'infest'. Harting embraced it particularly eagerly. It
even has an entry in his index: 'Wolf . . . districts for-
merly infested'. It is used at its most potent in this:

In 1848 there were living in Lochaber old people
who related from their predecessors, that when
all the country from the Lochie to Loch Erroch
[the River Lochy north of Fort William to Loch
Ericht south-west of Dalwhinnie] was covered by
a continuous pine forest, the eastern tracts upon
the Blackwater and the wild wilderness stretching
towards Rannach [Rannoch Moor] were so dense
and infested by the rabid droves, that they were
almost impassable.

. You have to admit it is a powerful image. His
Victorian audience would have nodded enthusiastic
agreement, and it has gone unchallenged into the literature of wolves. But let's see.

Suspending for the moment all rational thought
and scrutiny of the evidence, and assuming for the
sake of the argument that the last wolf really did die in
1743, the old people of Lochaber in 1848 were reaching back 105 years, so the oral testimony had lived
long enough to have been mangled by three if not four
generations, and as we have seen already, wolf stories
do not survive the passage of time with their credibility enhanced. Then there is the bit about Rannoch
Moor and tracts of pine forest so dense and infested
by the rabid droves that they were almost impassable.
Frank Fraser Darling, one of the best of the twentieth
century's scientist-naturalists, and a founder of the
Nature Conservancy Council, wrote in *The Highlands
and Islands* (1964), that Rannoch Moor 'may have
been extensively wooded *as recently as Roman times*'.
Darling's implication was that the most recent era of

woodland cover on the Moor was earlier rather than later. It certainly was, at the very least, far beyond the recall of the old people of Lochaber in the mid-nineteenth century, and for that matter far beyond the reach of knowledge that might have been handed down to them. What was handed down was a story-telling tradition, and that tradition demonised the wolf the length and breadth of the land.

Then there is the phrase 'infested by the rabid droves'. There are two things wrong there. One is that wolves do not move around in droves. They move in packs, or they move in twos and threes, or, as often as not, in summer, they move alone. A pack of European wolves is commonly anything between three and a dozen, exceptionally more than that, and, in summer, wolves rarely travel in packs at all. Packs defend their territories against neighbouring packs, and in a country the size of Scotland, territories would have covered several hundred square miles at least. So the possibility of droves of wolves does not exist, and it never did. Droves are simply not in the nature of wolves.

And then there is the implication that the only kind of droves you would encounter if you were foolish enough to attempt to force a passage through the impassable forest were rabid ones. Yes, there could well have been rabies in Highland Scotland three or four hundred years ago when Harting's wolves were infesting, and a rabid wolf is a serious problem for any creature unfortunate enough to encounter one, including human creatures. But so for that matter is a rabid bunny, a rabid sheepdog, or a rabid man. And there is no evidence to show that wolves were more susceptible to rabies than any other species. But there were always far fewer wolves than most other mammals in their landscape (for that is the nature of top predators – you can only have an abundance of predators when there is a superabundance of prey), so it becomes clear that Harting's casual use of the word 'rabid' is but one more ill-informed insult routinely hurled at the wolf's head. If, however, Harting used 'rabid', not to indicate rabies, but to characterise the wolf as 'furious, raging, madly violent in nature or behaviour' (alternative dictionary definition), the charge still sticks, for that too is unforgivable distortion of the reality of wolves. Harting waded knee-deep in the careless wolf prose of his contemporaries and his predecessors and represented it as more or less unquestionable fact.

Alas for the historical reputation of the wolf in Britain, much of the pigswill he brewed in the wolf chapters of his book (91 pages compared with 36 for wild boar, 18 for reindeer, 28 for beaver and 22 for bear – he enjoyed himself with wolves) has gone into the language. Worse, it is still quoted today, and not just by the gamekeeping fraternity where you might expect it, but also by elements within the conservation movement as casual with the truth as he was himself. His book is still widely available, thanks to a 1972 facsimile edition. The publishers would not have served the cause of wolves any worse by republishing *Little Red Riding Hood* and *The Three Little Pigs*.

One of his sources for the 'rabid droves' extract above was an 1848 book, *Lays of the Deer Forest*, by the brothers Sobieski-Stuart, two Germans who claimed to be the grandsons of Bonnie Prince Charlie.

The Victorians looked upon their claims of Jacobite aristocracy with a peculiar strain of romantic approval rather than as evidence that they might be complete fruitcakes, like most people who claim direct descent from the prince to this day, apparently secure in their belief that a Stuart will sit once again on the throne of Scotland. Aye, and hell will have frozen over. Harting lobs dollops of their grist into his mill without qualification or the mildest murmur of suspicion. But one of the most comprehensive and astute works on the history of Scotland's forests and the notion of the Great Wood of Caledon in particular, places the Sobieski-Stuarts where they belong, which is firmly in the fruitcake category. *The Native Woodlands of Scotland, 1500–2000*, by T.C. Smout, Alan R. MacDonald, and Fiona Watson (2005) observes:

> The Great Wood took on an altogether new lease of life in 1848 when the main ingredients of the modern myth were supplied by the Sobieski-Stuarts in their best-selling *Lays of the Deer Forest* . . . they claimed to be experts in the Gaelic past, and devised a compilation of poetry, aristocratic and romantic hunting stories, alleged clan histories, supposed folklore and natural history . . . They spoke of a Caledonia Silva, 'the great primeval cloud which covered the hills and plains of Scotland before they were cleared', and its 'skirt', a great forest filled with game and wolves that had occupied the Province of Moray, much of it surviving until recent times when ruthless and greedy modern man swept it away.

And after a passage that considered the climatic changes following the early Bronze Age and their consequences for the native forest, Smout, MacDonald and Watson write:

> In these circumstances, we would have greatly to reduce any estimates of woodland cover 5,000 years ago, perhaps by one-half, to arrive at a figure for 2,000 years ago. For a quarter of the land surface to have been wooded then would seem a possible figure. The present woodland cover of Scotland stands at 17 per cent, most of it plantation, and it is frequently urged upon us that the percentage should become much higher. There are many good arguments for planting trees in Scotland – to maintain employment, to give pleasure, to help carbon sequestration and to assist nature conservation. But it seems there may be fewer arguments from history than usually assumed, and none for restoring the fantastical Great Wood of Caledon.

Even if the figure for 2000 years ago was as much as a third of the land surface – so twice the extent of today's tree cover – it was quite unlike Harting's much-quoted portrait. It was not jungle, it was an airy northern forest flayed by Atlantic and Arctic winds. A restored national forest covering a third of the land-scape is a sublime ambition for twenty-first-century Scotland, but only if it is a good forest with much-reduced commercial plantation, only if we recruit the wolf to manage the deer in the forest and beyond it.

But myths die hard once the folk mind has embraced

them. Generations of writers regurgitated Harting (and therefore the Sobieski-Stuarts) and called it research. Only in the last few years has a more rigorous questioning of old sources begun. My own interest in such questioning is that a search for a new and more enlightened path through the impassable forests and the rabid droves will surely create a climate in which a fair hearing for the wolf is possible at last, and that as a result the wolf will be restored to its rightful place in the Scottish landscape.

It is also clear that Harting and many of his adherents wrote about the wolf and its Scottish habitat from a distance and in profound ignorance, a state of affairs that has contributed to myth-making and misunderstanding across almost every aspect of Scottish history. Harting quotes an earlier historian:

> Camden, whose *Britannia* was published in 1586, asserts that wolves at that date were common in many parts of Scotland, and particularly refers to Strathnavern. 'The county,' he says, 'hath little cause to brag of its fertility. By the reason of the sharpness of the air it is very thinly inhabited, and thereupon extremely infested with the fiercest of Wolves, which to the great damage of the county, not only furiously set upon cattle, but even upon the owners themselves, to the manifest danger of their lives.'

Thus Harting compounds the worst of felonies for a historian, or for that matter, a nature writer. Anyone who knows anything at all about the history of

Strathnaver in Sutherland will realise at once that neither Harting nor Camden had ever set foot in the place. A writer like David Craig, on the other hand, knows Strathnaver intimately, and paints a very different kind of landscape in his book *On the Crofters' Trail* (1990), the most powerful, vivid and compassionate reading of the Highland Clearances. The Clearances, to adapt Camden's wildly misdirected fiction, set upon the owners of those cattle nowhere more furiously than in Strathnaver. David Craig found lists of the evictees from Strathnaver in 1819, and there were 1,288 people on those lists, and that was the *second* clearing of Strathnaver. He unearthed the testimony of Angus Mackay, who had been cleared 'at the first burning in 1814', to the Napier Commission 70 years later. He said they had been 'reasonably comfortable' in their old home.

'You would see a mile or half a mile between every town; there were four or five families in each of these towns, and bonnie haughs between the towns, and hill pasture for miles, as far as they could wish to go. The people had plenty of flocks of goats, sheep, horses and cattle, and they were living happy . . . with flesh and fish and butter and cheese and fowl and potatoes and kail and milk too. There was no want of anything with them; and they had the Gospel preached to them at both ends of the strath . . . and in several other towns the elders and those who were taking to themselves to be following the means of grace were keeping a meeting once a fortnight – a prayer meeting amongst themselves –

and there were plenty gathering, so that the houses would be full.'

David Craig continues:

If anyone is inclined to dismiss this kind of thing as rose-tinted nostalgia, consider that the Sutherland estate itself reported that the 'general level of welfare' in Strathnaver was good.

What you realise as you walk all over the cleared lands of Scotland is that they were emptied because they were good places: that is, fit for the new large flocks of big southern sheep to feed on even in winter. Their greenness stands out today as though lit by some unfailing sunray among the brown heather moors. They are also picked out by pale blazes of the sheep, which still choose to browse there because ground that has once been cleared of stones, trenched for drainage, puddled by the hooves of animals, delved and fertilised over generations, maintains almost indefinitely its power to raise dense, juicy grass. If you stroke it, it feels tender. If you were blind, you would feel its resilience under your feet, as against the squelching or lumpy texture of the unimproved land round about – which also could have been improved by now, like the Yorkshire Dales or the Dolomite Alps, if crofting life had been allowed to go on evolving.

Strathnaver has been settled and made increasingly fertile at least since the broch builders, which is to say between 2,000 and 3,000 years.

So consider again Camden's assessment: 'The county hath little cause to brag of its fertility . . . it is very thinly inhabited and thereupon extremely infested with the fiercest of wolves, which to the great damage of the county not only furiously set upon cattle but even upon the owners themselves, to the manifest danger of their lives.' Consider the willingness with which Harting seized on it because it so suited his purpose of demonising the wolf, but not one word of it was true. If Harting paused once to consider how true it might or might not be, he kept his thoughts to himself. They were, of course, neither the first nor the last to misrepresent the Highlands in print from the twin blind spots of ignorance and distance. Some of the others, you might think, should have known better. As David Craig points out, when the Duchess of Sutherland married the Marquis of Stafford in 1785, 'at first they thought they had only 3,000 tenants – actually there were 15,000.'

The truth is that the Highland Clearances could never have happened if the land had not first been cleared of wolves. Flooding the glens with big, slow, dim-witted southern sheep would not have been such a realistic business proposition if the Highlands had still been infested with the rabid droves. So arguably the worst humanitarian disaster ever inflicted on the Highland people could never have been effected without first imposing unarguably its worst ecological disaster.

From the moment the last wolf died, nature in the Highlands – in all Scotland, all Britain – lurched out of control. It still is out of control, and it will remain out of control until the day the wild wolf is put back.

In a northern hemisphere country like this, if the wolf is in place everything in nature makes sense, but in the absence of wolves nothing in nature makes sense. In Scotland, instead of a top predator with the power to influence ecosystems, there are only eagles and a critically dwindling population of wild cats.

In the rest of Britain even these are absent, and there is nothing more predatory on the face of the land than a badger boar and a stroppy roebuck. Instead, your species and mine has persuaded itself that it can do the wolf's job, be the top predator and influence ecosystems. But we have added the un-wolf-like characteristic of trying to bully nature into submissive compliance. Nature resists, of course, but in an island country like ours, it has not yet invented a way to reintroduce the wolf. The next land-bridge to mainland Europe is still a few geological upheavals in the future, so it falls to us to put the wolf back, then be prepared to have it show us where we have gone wrong, how we might right those wrongs, and how to paint our mountains.

Meanwhile, Harting had been supping with the Sobieski-Stuarts again.

Towards the end of the sixteenth and beginning of the seventeenth centuries, large tracts of forests in the Highlands were purposely cut down or burned, as the only means of expelling the Wolves which there abounded.

If that was true, if large tracts of Highland forest were being cut down or burned, it is highly unlikely that the wolves which there abounded would have considered themselves expelled. Wolves don't need forests. They exist everywhere from the Arctic Circle to the Mediterranean, from Alaska to New Mexico, and in every conceivable habitat that such a geographical spread implies. Destroying a forest that held a wolf pack's entire territory would probably have made no bigger impact than to persuade the pack to redraw the boundaries of its territory, possibly to challenge a neighbouring pack, or to move to an area where there were no wolves. Bearing in mind that in the early seventeenth century the wolf was less than 200 years from extinction and had already suffered at least 500 years of hefty persecution, there would be plenty of wolfless country available to a disturbed pack. *If that was true . . .*

The Sobieski-Stuarts, quoted by Harting, had written:

> On the south side of Ben Nevis, a large pine forest, which extended from the western braes of Lochaber to the Black Water and the mosses of Rannach, was burned to expel the Wolves. In the neighbourhood of Loch Sloi, a tract of woods nearly twenty miles in extent was consumed for the same purpose.

Making generous allowance, his Lochaber-Rannoch claim might amount to four or five hundred square miles, which in turn might just amount to the territory of a single pack. The brothers' 'Loch Sloi' is a mystery, unless they meant tiny Loch Sloy near the north end of Loch Lomond, though it was hardly a nineteenth-century landmark. Yet that was enough for Harting to pronounce the demise of 'large tracts of forests in the Highlands'. *If that was true* . . .

But what was really happening in the Highlands at the turn of the seventeenth century? Smout, MacDonald and Watson write in *The Native Woodlands of Scotland* that in 1503 the Scottish Parliament announced that the country's timber supply was utterly destroyed:

> . . . probably reflecting at least the King's vexation in not being able to get his hands on the supplies he needed for his castles and ships. The tone of legislation in the next two centuries was consistently anxiety-ridden. Acts of 1535, 1607 and 1661 enjoined the planting and protection of timber . . . and Parliament in 1609, while stating that large woods had recently been discovered in the North was anxious that their value should not be frittered away.

So the presumption of King and Parliament was specifically against destroying more woodland, and would hardly have been likely to put the discomfort of the lieges at the sound of a howling wolf before the needs of the State.

As soon as you start to scratch the surface of what has passed for received wisdom about wolves throughout Scotland for at least the last 500 years, it cracks open, crumbles, and dematerialises into clouds of useless dust. Harting, alas, is the only one who collected some of its source material. It could have done with a more rigorous historian. Perhaps the most vivid evidence of just how lightly he scrutinised his sources emerges from Wales, and the story of the death of a wolf in the reign of King John, so the early part of the thirteenth century. He prefaces the story with the words, 'it is not at all unlikely that it is founded on fact.' Without further explanation he unleashes the following on his gullible readership:

Llewellyn, who was Prince of Wales in the reign of King John, resided at the foot of Snowdon, and, amongst a number of hounds which he possessed, had one of rare excellence which had been given to him by the King. [You get the sense already that it is not going to go well for the hound of rare excellence.] On one occasion, during the absence of the family, a Wolf entered the house; and Llewellyn, who first returned, was met at the door by his favourite dog, who came out, covered with blood, to greet his master. The prince, alarmed, ran into the house, to find his child's cradle overturned, and the ground flowing with blood. In a moment of terror, imagining the dog had killed the child, he plunged his sword into his body, and laid him dead on the spot. But, on turning up the cradle, he found his boy alive and sleeping by the side of the dead Wolf. The circumstance had such an effect on the mind of the prince, that he erected a tomb over the faithful dog's grave.

Where do you start with such a story? The Prince of Wales left a baby alone in the house with a hound for a guardian? He had no staff in his house? And if he had, they failed to hear a fight to the death between a hound and a wolf? And they let the hound answer the door to their returning master?

All of this presupposes, of course, that the wolf did indeed enter the house. The door of the house with the unguarded child was left open? Perhaps the wolf jumped onto the roof and went down the chimney? Then it walked through the many rooms until it found the one it wanted – the nursery with the cradle and the sleeping, unguarded child. It was about to clamp its jaws around the throat of the infant when the hound of rare excellence, the King's gift, chanced on the scene and – of course – killed the wolf.

'It is not at all unlikely that it is founded on fact . . .'

Likewise the Scalds of the North singing how the son of Siward gave the corpses of the French as a choice banquet for the wolves of Northumberland, no doubt. Two of the most durable indictments levelled against wolves in Britain were that they scavenged battlefields (hence the quotation at the start of this chapter) and dug out corpses from their graves. I heard the battlefield one perpetuated as recently as 2008 in the BBC's much-praised *History of Scotland* series. Presenter Neil Oliver, so scrupulous in his debunking of the myths that have enshrouded our human history for centuries, tossed it in as a footnote to an account of a twelfth-century battle involving a grandson of Malcolm Canmore somewhere down near the Mersey, observing that 'the corpses were picked over by wolves and carrion crows'. No other line in the whole series was that casual. There was no justification for it. It added nothing to the story he was telling other than the ancient image of a wolf with blood dripping from fangs.

It reminded me of a story told by the American nature writer Barry Lopez in his book *Of Wolves and Men* (1978). It concerned a visit to a school by a wolf and its handler as part of a wolf education programme. Before the visit the teacher had asked them to draw a wolf, with predictable results – fierce animals with big fangs. After the visit the teacher asked them to draw another picture. 'This time,' wrote Lopez, 'there were no fangs. All the pictures showed wolves with very big feet.'

It is possible that there were wolves at the aftermath of the battle. And carrion crows. And, foxes, ravens, buzzards, kites, cats, dogs . . . especially dogs, many dogs, which after all accompany men wherever they go, whatever they do. But there is no record of any of it. An assumption is made based on the repeatedly offered mantra of the ages, not on hard evidence offered by reliable historical record. A song composed by the Scalds of the North to honour Siward's victory would have lauded him as a warrior hero and belittled his enemies with all the venom at their disposal. Biologically, it would be as reliable as bluebirds over the white cliffs of Dover and nightingales singing in Berkeley Square. But no-one tried to palm off those examples of the songwriter's craft as historical evidence. The language used by Freeman in his *Northern Conquest* and quoted by Harting is the language of the Scalds who were paid to make their employer look good for the benefit of posterity. It was also their job to make the vanquished enemy look contemptible and unworthy of their place on the battlefield, so have them arrayed as a choice banquet for wolves, food for the lowest form of life! But when the Scalds of the North sang their song, did they know if wolves actually even liked human flesh? And did Freeman or Harting? And does anyone know now?

Wolves have preferences in what they eat. Scotland has never been short of deer, and for many millennia, these evolved with the wolf, and their movements and populations were shaped by wolves. And for many centuries cattle were the principal currency of the natives. In the last few hundred years before their extinction, killing deer would have put wolves in direct conflict with hunting kings and their royal hunting parks, and killing cattle would have put them in conflict with more or less everyone else. And before all that, the westward spread of Christianity had brought its demonising culture with it. The work of discrediting the wolf had begun and it lasted for more or less 2,000 years. It has still not quite died out, but at least now there are reintroduction programmes in America and Europe, reliable biological studies, hard evidence, wolf education programmes, and a growing presumption in favour of the animal as a benificent force in the land.

But some places are slower on the uptake than others, and nowhere is slower than Scotland, despite a European Union Habitats and Species Directive of 1992 compelling member governments to consider ways of reintroducing wolves. Putting the wolf back into Scotland could be done tomorrow, or indeed, with what's left of today, but the old lies and myths are well dug in and stubborn. Many farmers and landowners and estate managers are still constrained by short-term thinking and self-interest, and quite unwilling to give the wolf anything like a fair hearing. The wolf is still the devourer of children, the scavenger of battlefields, the grave-robber.

There are places all over the Highlands in particular with burial grounds on islands either in lochs or offshore – Loch Awe in Argyll, Loch Leven near Glencoe, Handa Island in Sutherland for example – whose existence is put down to the wolf's reputation as a grave-robber. Yet grave-robbing sounds too much like hard work to reach a source of carrion. It doesn't mean it never happened (and it would not have to happen often to establish the reputation – twice would have done it), if, say, the corpse was hastily buried in a shallow grave and without any kind of coffin. But island burial grounds are more likely to have originated in communities where good grazing land was at a premium: no point in wasting it on a field of the dead. The burial ground on Inishail in Loch Awe is still in use, incidentally, particularly by the Dukes of Argyll, more than 200 years after the last wolf died.

Both charges – the battlefield scavenger and the grave-robber – are unsubstantiated. They were levelled in a climate of wolf hatred. Such activities would have brought the wolf into quite unnecessary close contact with the two-legged creature it routinely went out of its way to avoid, and with good reason. The charges do not stand up to close historical or biological scrutiny. If the wolf was guilty as charged, it was the exception rather than the rule, whereas grave-robbing and battlefield scavenging was routinely practised by the species that levelled the charges – by people. And that species is still the only one that frequently kills children – people, and their pet dogs of course.

The rest of it was down to the myth-making of the centuries, to the songs of the Scalds of the North. The notion of the Rabid Droves was a fallacy.

CHAPTER 5
Last Wolf Syndrome

ONE OF THE BY-PRODUCTS of our age-old hostility towards the wolf is Last Wolf Syndrome. This phenomenon arose not simply out of a desire to cleanse the land of wolves, but also reflected the competitive element that thrives in any hunting culture. Reputations and rewards were at stake if people could be persuaded that the wolf you killed was the very last in that country, that county, that state, that district. In such a fevered climate, wolf hatred was heightened and Last Wolf stories began, you might say, to infest the land in droves. Last Wolf Syndrome seems to have originated in eastern Europe and spread rapidly, like all good infestations should. It engulfed Britain and effortlessly crossed the Atlantic with the early white settlers. As the stories spread it became clear that there were common ground rules. The wolf had to be hideously terrifying, preferably huge and black, and had to have killed someone vulnerable. The hunter had to be preternaturally gifted and heroic. At the end of the story, it was truth that was killed, a bloodied mess on the floor of a cave, usually with its head severed. Harting waded waist-deep in the gore of these stories.

An example of this occurs in an account of the slaughter of a remarkable wolf killed by one of the lairds of Chisolm in Gleann Chon-fhiadh, or the Wolves' Glen, a noted retreat of these animals in the sixteenth century.

The animal in question had made her den in a pile of loose rocks, whence she made excursions in every direction until she became the terror of the country. At length, the season of her cubs increasing her ferocity, and having killed some of the neighbouring people, she attracted the enterprise of the Laird of Chisolm and his brother, then two gallant young hunters, and they resolved to attempt her destruction. For this they set off alone from Strath Glass, and having tracked her to her den, discovered by her traces that she was abroad; but detecting the little pattering feet of the cubs in the sand about the mouth of the den, the elder crept into the chasm with his drawn dirk, and began the work of vengeance on the litter. While he was thus occupied, the Wolf returned, and infuriated by the expiring yelps of her cubs, rushed at the entrance, regardless of the younger Chisolm, who made a stroke at her with his spear, but such was her velocity that he missed her and broke the point of his weapon. His brother, however, met the animal as she entered, and being armed with the left-handed *lamhainn chruaidh*, or steel gauntlet, much used by the Highlanders and Irish, as the Wolf rushed open-mouthed upon him, he thrust the iron fist into her jaws, and stabbed her in the breast with his dirk, while his brother, striking at her flank with the broken spear, after a desperate struggle she was drawn out dead.

Gasp.

So, you get the gist. It's a run-of-the-mill example, with echoes of Skye, although I admit I did not see the stuff about the left-handed gauntlet coming. My inquiries on that particular subject drew a total blank. Whatever the *lamhainn chruaidh* may have been, it was far from 'characteristic of the Highlanders and Irish'. Indeed, it is far from clear what practical purpose it might have served other than the one in question – jamming into the open jaws of a wolf that happened to be running at you with its mouth open.

And then there was Sutherland. To this day, a cairn by the side of the A9 near Helmsdale lays claim to the killing of the last wolf in Sutherland, a deed done in Glen Loth, although there are rival claims from Assynt and Strath Halladale, all of them in the decade between 1690 and 1700. Inevitably, none died a natural or even a vaguely credible death, but if you believe in the notion of a folk mind that gathered and articulated these stories, it finally took leave of its senses in Glen Loth. Glen Loth is a bit-part player in the pageant of east Sutherland's mountainous landscape. Here, all the great valleys that drain into the North Sea are straths – Strath Fleet, Strath Brora, Strath of Kildonan – and in that company, Glen Loth is a skinny and unsung thoroughfare, unsung apart from the Pythonesque madness of its contribution to Last Wolf Syndrome. Its story is this (and see if you can spot the now familiar ingredients):

A Helmsdale man called Polson, his son, and another local lad, found a wolf's den in a small cave with a narrow entrance. Polson sent the boys in. Bones and

horns, feathers and eggshells littered the floor. Then
five or six cubs were found inside. The boys had been
told what to do. Soon Polson heard the death cries of
the cubs. Enter the female wolf 'raging furiously at the
cries of her young,' according to one of a number of
graphic accounts. It goes on:

> As she attempted to leap down, at one bound
> Polson instinctively threw himself forward and
> succeeded in catching a firm hold of the animal's
> long and bushy tail, just as the forepart of her body
> was within the narrow entrance of the cavern. He
> had unluckily placed his gun against a rock when
> aiding the boys in their descent, and could not now
> reach it. Without apprising the lads below of their
> imminent peril, the stout hunter kept a firm grip of
> the wolf's tail, which he wound round his left arm,
> and although the maddened brute scrambled and
> twisted and strove with all her might to force her-
> self down to the rescue of her cubs, Polson was just
> able with the exertion of all his strength to keep her
> from going forward. In the midst of this singular
> struggle, which passed in silence, his son within the
> cave, finding the light excluded from above asked
> in Gaelic, 'Father, what is keeping the light from
> us?' 'If the root of the tail breaks,' replied he, 'you
> will soon know that.'

And, of course, the hunter prevailed, jamming the
she-wolf into the rocks, unsheathing his knife and stabbing her so often that at last 'she was easily dragged
back and finished'.

If you had never waded through yards of last wolf stories but encountered instead only the handful that caught the wolf by the tail, you could be forgiven for thinking there was something in it. If on the other hand, you had done the required wading, you would be utterly convinced that there is less than nothing in it. But I went in search of greater authority, and found it in Erik Zimen's book, *The Wolf*. Zimen was German, grew up in Sweden, got a doctorate for his work in wolf ecology from the University of Kiel, did post-doctorate work with the famed biologist Konrad Lorenz in Bavaria, then led a trail-blazing wolf conservation project in Italy's Abruzzi National Park. In the throes of all that he encountered many wolf stories from many countries, and found countless variations on the same few well-worn themes:

> There is no lack of such incredible stories. A celebrated German hunting writer, for instance, describes quite seriously an incident said to have happened in central Sweden in 1727. A minister . . . heard the howling of wolves from a wolf pit he had dug. (Just imagine trapped wolves 'making their dreadful lonely voices heard,' as it says in the book.) In trying to kill one of the six wolves that ferociously bared their teeth at him, he fell into the pit himself, but miraculously the wolves did not tear him to pieces but used his back to climb out of the pit and escape.

Another echo of Skye.

Many stories keep cropping up in different areas in a similar form. There is the story of . . . the solitary individual who is attacked by wolves on a cold winter night. He defends himself with his sword and succeeds in killing or wounding several of them. The rest withdraw and the man puts his sword back in its sheath. But that is a mistake, because the wolves attack again, and this time the bloodstained sword is frozen in the sheath, with the result that only a few remnants of the man are left, as well as the sword, of course, as evidence of the tragic event.

There is a striking resemblance in stories coming from many areas. The Russian version – the troika pursued by wolves on a winter night – has been repeated a thousand times. Its North American counterpart has the hero alone with his dog at a campfire and he has to defend himself against attacking wolves by swinging his cudgel. All these stories happen on a winter night and in all of them the ammunition runs out, but the hero's courage, resourcefulness, and strength enable him to win against all odds.

In the course of my work with wolves I have heard or read a large number of such stories, told by aged sportsmen in the Carpathians or German ex-servicemen who fought in Russia. Many of them have exactly the same plot and can thus be dismissed as unimaginative reproduction of the standard repertoire of aggressive tactics attributed to the wolf. Others, though sometimes more imaginative, are so full of phoney details about wolf behaviour that they are incredible . . . In the great majority of these stories there is a complete lack of critical questioning.

So the tail-pullers are simply symptomatic of a story-telling tradition that has left its spoor all over Europe. When it crossed the Atlantic with the early settlers, it cut no ice with native Americans, who knew better and had inherited an ancient relationship that accorded the wolf the status of an equal. The American nature writer, Barry Lopez, touched on that relationship in *Of Wolves and Men*:

> The Nunamiut Eskimos, the Naskapi Indians of Labrador, the tribes of the northern plains of the North Pacific Coast . . . are all, in a sense, timeless. Even those tribes we can converse with today because they happen to live in our own age, are timeless; the ideas that surface in conversation with them (even inside a helicopter at 2,000 feet) are ancient ideas . . . And the life they lead, you notice, tagging along behind them as they hunt, really is replete with examples of the way wolves do things. Over thousands of years, Eskimos and wolves have tended to develop the same kind of efficiency in the Arctic.

And Zimen wrote:

> Stories told by aged Eskimos show a surprising knowledge of the ecology and behaviour of the wolf. They too hunted it for its pelt and later for bounty paid by the government for dead wolves.

But, like Indians, they do not share the hatred of the wolf that is so evident in other societies. Their idea of the wolf coincides to a large extent with ours of the present day. There are differences only on a few points. According to the Eskimo, the wolf is not only highly intelligent and social, which rouses their admiration, but frequently acts with insight and deliberation – an idea that after four years' work in the Abruzzi no longer seems to me to be so completely off the mark.

As wolf populations began to dwindle towards local extinctions, then, the European storytelling tradition acquired the extra edge of Last Wolf Syndrome. I was intrigued by two accounts of the killing of the last one in Scotland. The first story, claiming it for Perthshire, attracted me because it is so matter-of-fact. The other, giving the honour to a certain MacQueen and placing it in the strath of the River Findhorn, caught my attention because its complete absence of credibility has not stopped it from becoming widely accepted as authentic. The Perthshire killing was said to have happened at the Pass of Killiecrankie, where in 1680 Sir Ewan Cameron of Lochiel reputedly shot what was popularly believed at the time to be the last wolf in Scotland, an event for which Harting had unearthed an intriguing footnote:

In the sale catalogue of the 'London Museum' which was disposed of by auction in April 1818, there is the following entry: 'Lot 832. Wolf – a noble animal in a large glass case. The last Wolf killed in Scotland by Sir E. Cameron.'

So at least it seems clear that a wolf was killed there, and there is the refreshing absence of preposterous detail or hunter-heroics. Cameron of Locheil simply shot it and had it stuffed. In 1818, staff at the London Museum clearly believed they were selling the last wolf killed in Scotland (not the last wolf, note, merely the last one killed), and bear in mind that this was still eight years before Thomas Dick Lauder published an extraordinary account of the intrepid MacQueen and his exploits up the Findhorn in 1743. Until Lauder's book was published in 1830, there had been no challenger to Locheil's claim to fame, therefore it is quite possible that there was no challenger, because MacQueen never did kill a wolf up the Findhorn in 1743 or any other year.

Before I went to up to the Findhorn in search of MacQueen, then, I headed for the Pass of Killiecrankie just off the A9 and just north of Pitlochry. The Pass is now in the care of the National Trust for Scotland as a surviving example of ancient native woodland and as the setting of a famous battle in 1689 between Jacobite and Hanoverian forces, the Jacobites led by Viscount Dundee, whose army included none other than the same Sir Ewan Cameron of Locheil in its ranks. The Jacobites' spectacular victory was marred only by the death of the man known as Bonnie Dundee.

Tourism has moved in. There is no avoiding the visitor centre and its walk-this-way regime, nor the interpretative material that seems to assume the average visitor has a mental age of five. But trees still throng the steep flanks of the pass, mostly oaks, although despite the tourist leaflet explanation that the name Killiecrankie

means aspen wood there are precious few aspens. A
quiet midweek autumn day with a good seasonal blaze
in the foliage and with the River Garry preferably in
boisterous spate offer the best circumstances for outwitting the tourist industry here and coming to terms with
some sense of a place with a continuous woodland evolution over 8,000 years. The steepness of the gorge has
saved the trees from the twin fates of so much ancient
woodland – overgrazing by sheep and deer and over-
exploitation by people. Catch it early with a morning
mist swithering above the gorge and have the epochal
stillness of the trees vie with the turbulence of the river.
Then, perhaps, you can briefly believe in wolves.

Perhaps. But so much has gone from places like Kil-
licrankie. It has a conservationist's fence thrown round
it because it is so small, a rearguard action whose best
endeavour is to sustain a remnant. And wolves need
more than remnants, they need space, hundreds of
square miles of it for a single pack. I decided to try
the visitor centre as a kind of last resort. Perhaps there
were archives, insights.

I was very courteously received. I explained my
mission. Yes, they were aware of the story of Ewan
Cameron of Locheil and the last wolf in Perthshire,
and there used to be something about it in the audio-
visual programme, but that had been redone recently
and the wolf story was edited out. I wondered why out
loud. There was no answer. We leafed through some
folders of documents and drew a blank. The woman
who handled my inquiry said she would go and consult
the centre manager. She was back in a few minutes. Her
boss's verdict was that Locheil had indeed shot the last

Perthshire wolf there in 1680, 'but the last one of all was killed near Inverness in 1720 by an old woman who hit it with a frying pan'.

I offered my polite thanks and left. I sat in the car in the visitor centre car park in the rain with a cup of visitor centre coffee and laughed out loud. This is what our wilderness heritage has become. Millions of years of evolution, much of that evolution shaped by the presence of wolves just as they continue to shape the evolution of those northern hemisphere landscapes where they still hold sway, and all that legacy has become a footnote, a throwaway line about an old woman and a frying pan. I remembered something my dear old friend Marion Campbell of Kilberry wrote on the subject of trying to extract a sense of the past from the myths we are left with:

> Those myths survive only in the faintest echoes, all
> meaning lost, their outer shells turned into comic
> tales. They stir in our deepest subconscious like fish
> in a pool, the last link in a chain of oral learning.

For you will search the oldest written texts we know and all those that followed until Scotland lost interest in its absent wolf over a hundred years ago, but you will search in vain for the real living wolf, for it is not there. Myths survive but 'only in the faintest echoes, all meaning lost, their outer shells turned into comic tales.' The stories – the countless stories – about how innumerable 'last wolves' met their fate are exactly that – stories. Those stories and many others that paint the wolf as a bloody-fanged disciple of the Devil punctuate the face of our landscape from the northmost Scotland to southmost England. Each one is nothing more than a headstone to the passing, not of a wild animal, but of an oral tradition. The real wild wolf, that may or may not have lived around the edges of the storytellers' lives, was never allowed to put in an appearance in the stories. And none of them is more damning of the whole absurd tradition than the one about the old woman and the frying pan.

It was set in that hotbed of anti-wolf propaganda that was Strath Glass. Or perhaps it was just that they bred generations of supremely accomplished storytellers there. And it involved one of the classic ingredients identified by Erik Zimen – the solitary figure in a winter landscape, just before Christmas. And of course it too proved irresistible to Professor Harting:

> Another story is on record of a Wolf killed by a woman . . . near Strui [Struy] on the north side of Strath Glass. She had gone to Strui a little before Christmas to borrow a griddle (a thick circular plate of iron, with an iron loop handle and one side for lifting, and used for baking bread). Having procured it, and being on her way home, she sat down upon an old cairn to rest and gossip with a neighbour, when suddenly a scraping of stones and rustling of dead leaves were heard, and the head of a wolf protruded from a crevice at her side. Instead of fleeing in alarm, however, 'she dealt him such a blow on the skull with the full swing of her iron discuss, that it brained him on the stone which served for his emerging head.'

This tradition was probably one of the latest in the district, and seems to have belonged to a period when the Wolves were near their end.

So it was with a heavy and sceptical heart that I turned north for the valley of the Findhorn River in search of the spoor of MacQueen and what so many writers over so many centuries have been only too willing to acknowledge was the last wolf of all.

CHAPTER 6
The Findhorn

'Every district,' says Stuart in his 'Lays of the Deer Forest,' 'has its "last" Wolf," and there were probably several which were later than that killed by Sir Ewan Cameron. The "last" of Strath Glass was killed at Gusachan according to tradition "at no very distant period" . . . and the last of the Findhorn and also (as there seems every reason to believe) the last of the species in Scotland, at a place between Fi-Giuthas and Pall-a-chrocain, and according to popular chronology no longer ago than 1743.'

– James Edmund Harting, *British Animals Extinct Within Historic Times* (1880)

THE VICTORIANS inflicted a regime of wildlife slaughter on Highland Scotland. It co-existed alongside a peculiarly persuasive strain of romanticism for which Sir Walter Scott was more or less single-handedly responsible, and the London government's grim imposition of the Highland Clearances on the natives, whom they replaced with huge flocks of sheep and great herds of red deer. This heady combination of forces instilled a doctrine of hatred for anything in nature that wore a hook to its beak or talons to its feet, or anything that used tooth and claw to go about its daily business. In such a climate, it is not hard to envisage the Victorian mindset's reverence for the slaying of the last wolf by a heroic hunter a hundred years before. What a fine example from recent history to uphold for the benefit of the modern Victorian stalker! A celebrity hunter whose superhuman strength and astounding heroism had accounted for the last dreadful child-slaying, devil-black vestige of the Highland wolf was surely a story worth telling and re-telling and handing down the generations like an old family bible, to be believed in its entirety because no-one dared to disbelieve.

I decided to visit the River Findhorn in search of 'a place between Fi-Giuthas and Pall-a-chrocain' to see what they might make of the story there today, if they made anything of it at all, and to see if the last wolf of the Findhorn was any better served by posterity than the last wolf of Perthshire was at Killiecrankie. Fi-Giuthas has vanished from the map if it was ever there, but Harting's occasional use of Gaelic, whether in place names or slivers of conversation, swithers between actual and approximate Gaelic words and phonetic stabs at the sound of the words. *Giuthas* is a Gaelic word meaning pine tree. *Fi* could be a phonetic attempt at rendering *fiadh*, the Gaelic for a deer, or *feidh*, the plural, and what he wrote down as Fi-Giuthas was a pinewood known for its deer, in which case time has erased it from the landscape as well as the map. His Pall-a-chrocain is there though, rendered on modern maps as Ballachrochin, which is near enough given the Gaelic language's tendency to make the letter 'b' at the beginning of a word sound like 'p'. *Baile* is the Gaelic for a township and the source of most 'Bal' place names, and *crobhcan* means anything crooked or twisted or bent into a roughly-formed 'S' shape, which describes the River Findhorn at Ballachrochin more or less perfectly.

The Findhorn rises in the Monadhliath, 20 miles south of Inverness, and flows more or less north-east to the Moray Firth at Findhorn Bay. It is a truly beautiful river, but it is eclipsed in the thoughtless gaze of twenty-first-century tourism by its near neighbour, the Spey, which also rises in the Monadhliath and flows along a parallel course to meet the sea at Spey Bay, but is longer, wider and many times more famous, a world-renowned focal point of the whisky industry, a salmon river of distinction and a magnet for tourism. Its broad strath and the many communities along its banks service the Cairngorms National Park, and good roads accompany it over much of its length on both banks. The Findhorn, by comparison, ploughs its furrow through a landscape more or less empty of people, and mostly has to make do with estate tracks, a solitary whisky distillery at Tomatin, and the exquisite hidden treasure that is Dulsie Bridge built by General Wade.

Its upper reaches flow through Strath Dearn, which may explain a curious reference in Harting's book that had me baffled for months and sent me on an extravagant wild-goose chase, for he had written that 'in the districts where Wolves last abounded, many traditions of their history and haunts have descended to our time. The greatest number preserved in one circle were in the neighbourhood of Strath Earn.'

The Earn flows east out of Loch Earn through the comparatively douce landscapes around Comrie and Crieff, then wends a decidedly Lowland course to join the Tay east of Perth. It is a landscape I have known more or less all my life, and not once had I come across a wolf tradition there. So I set about scouring known historical sources for signs of an infestation of wolves. None revealed itself. Then I started to study maps of the Findhorn, a landscape with which I was relatively unfamiliar, and I found Strath Dearn. Harting or his publisher or the publisher of the twentieth-century reprint had made a simple typo.

I decided to approach MacQueen's country from the north, circling stealthily (like a wolf, as I fancied it) east of the River Findhorn by way of the vast spaciousness of a high moorland B-road that climbs north out of Carrbridge and breasts the 1,300-feet contour amid a small clutch of craggy hilltops, one of which is called Creag a'Ghiuthas. It must be several miles from there to the nearest pine tree today, but perhaps when the landscape was named, that high moorland sprawl was also a high pinewood sprawl and the pinewood known for its deer, and the whole wild landscape of the Findhorn known for its wolves.

This is a big landscape by Scottish standards, the wild moorland miles to east and west, lower-lying woodland to the north where the land starts to dip towards the distant sea, and to the south there are sightlines into the northern Cairngorms to put your

heart in your mouth. From many compass points
the distant Cairngorms fold into each other and create the deceptively unimpressive aspect of a slabby
plateau. People have died being unimpressed by
their first sight of the Cairngorms. But from the high
ground to the north they mass awesomely into an
army of mountains, sliced into battalions by the great
troughs of Gleann Einich and the Lairg Ghru. There
is no doubting their scale, no escaping their intimidat-
ing aspect. Standing on the small plateau summit of
Creag Eairaich and looking around, something fundamental changed in me. The possibility that I had so
fondly entertained for so long of reintroducing wolves
into my own country suddenly acquired a ferociously
practical reality.

'Look at this place,' I said aloud to no-one. 'How
can anyone believe that there should *not* be wolves
here?'

The sheer scope and uncompromising wildness of
the landscape in almost every direction imposed itself
on my solitude with a quite unexpected forcefulness. It
had never been on my preferred list of wolf-reintroduc-
tion landscapes, a short list headed by Rannoch Moor,
but it had just imposed itself on my list quite uninvited.
Uniquely in the course of these journeys among old
wolf haunts I toyed with the notion that I had been
led there. It is, of course, the most unscientific of arguments, and it was preached to a converted audience of
one by the audience itself, but science is not the only
valid consideration in a phenomenon as emotive as the
place of wolves in a landscape.

Science can be ponderous and myopic and blinkered

by both history and politics. For example, as I write
this a small group of Norwegian beavers is being
released from quarantine into the wild in Knapdale,
Argyll, a timid attempt at reintroduction hamstrung
with safeguards and qualifications and tags and radio-
collars, a five-year study and a threat by the scheme's
partners to cull or sterilise the beavers if things go
wrong in the eyes of those influential vested interests
who have opposed the scheme from the start. It has
taken 15 years to get us to this point, thanks largely
to ponderous, blinkered, myopic science and less than
inspirational politics. It is that long ago now since I
made a radio programme on the subject, and a senior
official at Scottish Natural Heritage said on air that
we would have beavers back in Scotland in two years.
Science and politics had other ideas. If it has been so
ponderous a process for beavers, which eat nothing
more precious to us than willow bark, it is not easy to
be optimistic that science and politics will fast-track
wolf reintroduction onto the agenda.

But I stood on the summit of Creag Eairaich and a
peculiar sense of purpose attended the moment. Perhaps in retrospect it was not so surprising, for my life
at that point was consumed in the process of making
this book, fighting the wolf's corner, criss-crossing the
country in pursuit of the elusive sense of them in my
native landscapes more than 200 years after they vanished off the face of my portion of the earth, borrowing
from the experiences of other countries where the presence of the wolf is unbroken or where it has found its
own way back or where it has been put back. And I was
closing in on the spoor of the most outrageous of all

Scotland's wolf traditions, the one that had been regurgitated so often over so many years that it had acquired a specific significance as the moment when Scotland was finally rid of its wolves, and because it had a date it had become history. Yet, curiously enough, Harting of all people had paused in the face of this landscape and made an uncharacteristically realistic assessment of it, considering the wildly extravagant use to which he was putting it, although whether he was ever here is less than clear or likely.

> The district . . . was well calculated to have given harbour to the last of a savage race. All the country round his haunt was an extent of wild and desolate moorland hills, beyond which, in the west, there was retreat to the vast wilderness of the Monadhliath, an immense tract of desert mountains utterly uninhabited, and unfrequented except by summer herds and herdsmen, but when the cattle had retired, abundantly replenished with deer and other game, to give ample provision to the 'wild dogs'.

And if he had added the Cairngorms into the equation, here was – and still is – an area of around 600 square miles that could have accommodated – and still could – a pack of wolves. One pack, mind you, not an infestation.

I crossed the Findhorn at Dulsie Bridge, a spectacular example of General Wade's bridge-building capabilities as he stamped the land with military roads in the aftermath of Culloden; the whorls of the London government's fingerprints were unmistakable. It was the beginning of the subjugation of the Highlands. The Clearances would be the end of the process. But for all that it represents, Dulsie Bridge was and still is an exquisite marriage of architecture and engineering and the stonemason's art.

I began to close in on MacQueen by way of a furtive, narrowing, deteriorating road that tiptoed through thick woodland. Suddenly the road slipped the leash of the trees and dropped to the river. Pheasants and partridges scattered on both sides, or simply ran ahead of the car for hundreds of yards. The wolves would have loved them. Clear views of the river confirmed the map's diagnosis, that the next five or six upstream miles of the Findhorn were folded deep in a sinuous canyon. About halfway up and on the far side of the river was a tiny square marked Ballachrochin. In my mind's eye I saw a small and roofless stone ruin, walls caved in, a discernible doorway; perhaps the gables still stood, and an owl or a kestrel or a raven nested in the ghost of chimney.

I weighed up the possibilities. Bulldozed roads climbed the far hillside, and there was an estate bridge near Drynachan Lodge. If I could walk up that road to get above the canyon, I could look down on Ballachrochin, and scatter the bones of a 260-year-old story on the twenty-first-century landscape. I met a keeper outside his house, explained my mission, my wolf project, my interest in MacQueen and the story in which he had the starring role, and asked if I might use the bridge and walk up the bulldozed road across the glen. It was a Sunday, and I didn't expect there to be anyone shooting up there.

My request was met with a quiet smile, and an assurance that I would not find many wolves at Ballachrochin. If he knew the story of MacQueen, he expressed not the slightest interest in it. He was more concerned about where I walked.

'If you don't mind, I'd rather you stayed this side of the river. We have a great many birds up on the other side. But if you park at the end of the tarmac road you'll have a lovely walk up this side and you'll see all you need to see of Ballachrochin.'

And so I did. I climbed high above the river on an easy track, then abandoned it to follow the upper edge of the canyon. Upstream, the Findhorn wound its way south-west, catching sunlight and shadow, dodging in and out of sight, until one last far-off blue-black mountainside terminated the view. Beyond that mountainside the unseen A9 would be clattering indifferently by as it curved round the lower reaches of Strathdearn.

At that stage, I was quietly pleased with my strategy. I had a late lunch on a high, heathery seat in the sunshine. The river uncoiled far below round a flat and grassy bowl, beyond which patches of old birchwood dropped hints of the old woodland character of the place. A small and derelict stone house stood in the middle of the flat green sward. I guessed it was as prone to flooding as any house in the Highlands. Anyway, it was at least a hundred years too modern for MacQueen.

Sunlight was highlighting some strange patterns high up on the far hillside. I put the binoculars on them and found . . . fields. What on earth were they planting away up there? Then I realised that whatever it was, its principle purpose was to provide cover for thousands and thousands of partridges and pheasants. I could imagine the neighbourhood golden eagles queuing up over such a hillside. I could also imagine there might be a degree of hostility on this particular estate to the notion of wolves returning to the site of their legendary last stand, and perhaps that had explained the keeper's unenthusiastic response.

I walked on, still heading south-west, slowly unravelling the river, coil after coil, half drunk on the honeyed smell of the heather and the sun and the play of light and shadow on near and far hillsides, and the dance of it on the water. Then I saw clusters of chimneys protruding from distant trees. But they were not decrepit chimneys, and they were not broken-down stone, and they were not the chimneys of a small and roofless ruin. There were also rather a lot of them. The building they served was new and white and shielded from prying eyes by trees and it was very big. Whatever may have stood there in 1743, the twenty-first-century Ballachrochin is a substantial mansion house.

I felt defeated. The estate was modern and forward-thinking and looked prosperous, and seemed utterly indifferent to its old claim to fame. Highland tourism routinely makes a meal of the landscape's association with historical events: not here. There is no plaque, no notice, no leaflet, no hint that a giant called MacQueen had ever set foot here, far less killed a wolf, *the* wolf, the last wolf, the very last Last Wolf. For no good reason at all now that I think about it,

I had expected to find a glen like so many others in the Highlands, beleaguered by its past, and shorn of its potential by 150 years of over-dependence on too many sheep and too many deer and too few natives. Instead there were clusters of white chimneys and thousands of partridges. And here and there along the river, expensive four-wheel-drive this-and-thats ferried anglers out to the choice beats. From time to time the voices of the anglers, a touch too strident for my comfort, rode the thermals up to where I sat. And suddenly nothing fitted.

What now? I had had MacQueen in my sights all the time I was travelling north, all the way from the southern Highland Edge to Carrbridge to the revelation of Creag Eairlaich, the slow drive over the Wade bridge and through the trees. Ballachrochin was to be the gunfight at the OK Corral, the duel in the sun where I would shoot holes in MacQueen's reputation. But Ballachrochin was doubly shut in – by its Victorian tree planting and the river's canyon walls. There was no-one to shoot at, and my mission seemed ludicrous. What did I expect to find – a seven-feet-long rusting iron bedstead standing in the ruins?

But I still believed the last wolf story was fiction, like all the others, that MacQueen was just one more fictional component in a fictional story with a fictional dialogue; that he had a walk-on part in a fake history. Yet somehow I had still thought I was going to nail him in his own backyard. But if he was a fiction he had no back yard, and Ballachrochin was only a storyteller's stage set. The possibility of wolves had been palpable on the summit of Creag Eairlaich. There had been that extraordinary sense of being led, of destination. There, I had been working with reality, with a living landscape where real wolves had lived and could live again. Then I allowed myself to be distracted by the ghost of a man who may never have lived at all.

But MacQueen was still the key to disproving the last wolf story, and it was necessary to disprove it so that history would have to look again at the place of the wolf in Scotland and make a more thoughtful assessment. And that would surely assist the cause of the wolf's return. But how do you begin to disprove a story set in 1743, whose central character may or may not have existed, a story whose landscape setting treats it with an indifferent shrug?

I drove to Inverness in the rain, spent several hours in a public library reading turgid local histories and old wildlife books and romanticised explorations of Highland landscapes written by obscure hacks a hundred years ago, looking in vain for some indisputable fact or flimsy hint that would allow me to lay to rest MacQueen and his last wolf and 1743 and all that once and for all. All I found were Harting quotes and Harting rewrites, and such a sniffy indifference from the solitary member of staff that the morning settled on me like a personal rain cloud.

I found a quiet bar and considered once again the gospel according to Harting in some detail.

The last of their race was killed by MacQueen of Pall-a-chrocain, who died in the year 1797, and was the most celebrated 'carnach' of the Findhorn for an unknown period.

I don't know what a *carnach* is. The only meaning I can find for the word is 'a rocky place' which is not what Harting was looking for. The implication is that he had a bit of a reputation 'for an unknown period' which is as meaningless a character reference as I have ever encountered.

> Of gigantic stature, six feet seven inches in height, he was equally remarkable for his strength, courage, and celebrity as a deer-stalker, and had the best 'long dogs' or deer hounds in the country.

I remembered Erik Zimen's appraisal of so many wolf stories from Europe: 'All these stories happen on a winter night . . . the hero's courage, resourcefulness, and strength enable him to win against the odds.' I wished I had his book with me in the bar, but I did not. I only had Harting's.

> One winter's day [Zimen noted it was almost always a winter day] he received a message from the Laird of MacIntosh that a large 'black beast', supposed to be a Wolf, had appeared in the glens, and the day before killed two children, who with their mother were crossing the hills from Calder [possibly Cawdor], in consequence of which a 'Tainchel' or 'gathering' to drive the country was called to meet at a tryst above Fi-Giuthas, where MacQueen was invited to attend with his dogs. He informed himself of the place where the children had been killed, the last tracks of the Wolf, and the conjectures of his haunt, and promised assistance.

All the ingredients of the European wolf fable are in place: it is winter, the wolf is large and black, a figure is crossing the winter landscape (the addition of two children is an adornment), the hunter is huge and possessed of great strength and will surely prevail so that the wolf-oppressed population can rest easy in their beds again, and walk the hills alone in winter with impunity and with their vulnerability unexploited. Harting ploughed on:

In the morning the 'Tainchel' has long assembled, and MacIntosh waited with impatience, but MacQueen did not arrive. His dogs and himself were, however, auxiliaries too important to be left behind, and they continued to wait until the best of a hunter's morning was gone, when at last he appeared, and MacIntosh received him with an irritable expression of disappointment.

'Ciod a a chabhag?' ('What was the hurry?') said he of Pall-a-chrocain.

MacIntosh gave an indignant retort, and all present made some impatient reply.

MacQueen lifted his plaid and drew the black, bloody head of the Wolf from under his arm!

'Sin e dhuibh!' ('There it is for you!') said he, and tossed it on the grass in the midst of the surprised circle.

There then follows MacQueen's account of the deed in his own words, complete with Harting's helpful if approximate translations, and if you were tempted to afford the story any shred of credibility thus far, credibility now dies with the last black, child-slaying beast of the Findhorn:

> 'As I came through the slochk (i.e. ravine) by east the hill there,' said he as if talking of some every-day occurrence, 'I foregathered wi' the beast. My long dog there turned him. I buckled wi' him and dirkit him, and syne whuttled his craig (i.e., cut his throat) and brought awa' his countenance for fear he might come alive again, for they are very precarious creatures.'

Suddenly the Gaelic-speaking MacQueen is reduced to a single word of Gaelic (Harting opts for a phonetic rendering of *slochd*, meaning a pass rather than a ravine) and starts havering away in Lowland Scots, not just Lowland Scots but something that reads as if it was trying desperately to be a piece of dialogue from a novel by Sir Walter Scott, but not quite carrying it off. Undemanding posterity has put the two events together – the 1743 slaying and the direct speech of MacQueen – but as Harting points out (and many subsequent writers have chosen to ignore for it doesn't half ruin the story) the whole thing was written down by Sir Thomas Dick Lauder in 1830 in his account of the Moray floods of the previous year.

I closed Harting's book for the last time, hoping against hope that I would have no further use of it for a long, long time. The colossal folly of the Victorians freed them from the reality of the natural world to such an extent that they had clasped to their collective bosom such a grotesquely mangled representation of what – if anything at all – happened here. I sipped my beer and looked out at the rain thudding against the window of the bar in long diagonal streaks, reducing Inverness to a grey blur. And the passage of time, I thought, has reduced the reputation of the wolf to much the same thing.

As I drove home I thought about Lauder, about whom I knew next to nothing. He was a minor Scottish writer, and like all minor Scottish writers of the time he lived in the colossal shadow of Scott. Scott had published 21 novels between 1814 and 1828. Scotland, much of the rest of Britain, and – crucially – Queen Victoria were obsessed by him. He was a renowned manipulator of historical events, who, among other things, had transformed Rob Roy into something he never was in real life and created a landscape called the Trossachs; both these inventions live on in the twenty-first century. W.H. Murray, whose *Rob Roy – His Life and Times* was published in 1982, has written:

> In righting the wrong done to Rob Roy's name by Scott, and by the historians whom he and others followed, I have found Rob Roy to be of stronger character than the early writers had imagined. Their works on Rob Roy require so much correction and refutation that few readers would wish to plough a way through the quagmire.

And then I had what Hemingway called 'one of those unsound but illuminating thoughts you have

when you have been sleepless or hungry', and as it happened, at that point I was both. It was this: MacQueen
was Lauder's Rob Roy. A few days later I was in the
Scottish Library in Edinburgh.

'Sir Thomas Dick Lauder, Bart., of Grange and Fountainhall, FRSE' is the byline on his best-known book,
The Great Moray Floods of 1829. Grange is a posh
part of Edinburgh, Fountainhall is near Haddington
in East Lothian, and FRSE indicates a Fellow of the
Royal Society of Edinburgh. Sir Thomas was minor
aristocracy, with roots deeply embedded in Edinburgh
society, who numbered the architect William Playfair
(designer of the National Gallery of Scotland), the
ubiquitous Lord Cockburn, and almost inevitably Sir
Walter Scott among his acquaintances. But he spent
much of his adult life at Relugas in Forres near the
Moray coast, and was there to witness the frighten-
ing floods of 1829. His life was rich and varied, and
his achievements included many commendable public
works for people less fortunate than himself, but he
did rather flatter himself that he could write. He was
so in thrall to Scott that when he tackled a historical
romance based on the life of Alexander Stewart, Earl
of Buchan, Lord of Badenoch, the son of Robert II,
and the fourteenth century's most charming Highland
thug, otherwise known as the Wolf of Badenoch, he
felt compelled to issue a curious third-person dis-
claimer in a foreword spattered with code names for
Scott:

The author has been accused of being an imita-
tor of the Great Unknown. In his own defence

he must say that he is far from being wilfully so. In truth, his greatest anxiety has been to avoid intruding profanely into the sacred haunts of the Master Enchanter. But let it be remembered that the Mighty Spirit of the Magician has already so filled the labyrinth of Romance that it is not easy to venture within its precincts without feeling his influence; and to say that, in exploring the intricacies of these Wizard paths, one is to be denounced for unwittingly treading upon those flowers which have been pressed by his giant foot, amounts to a perfect prohibition of all entrance there.

By the time he started to write *The Great Moray Floods of 1829* then, he had already acknowledged the helpless nature of his thraldom to the admittedly overwhelming influence of Scott. In Lauder's *Wolfe of Badenoch*, that conspicuously affected final 'e' appears to serve no purpose other than to differentiate between his hero and the four-legged wolf that becomes embroiled in mortal combat (and loses, of course) with one of the book's other characters. It is educational to savour some of the language that colours his account of the fight:

He saw an enormous wolf making towards him, the oblique and sinister eyes of the animal flashing fire, his jaws extended and tongue lolling out . . .
The panting and frothy jaws and long sharp tusks of the infuriated beast . . .
The muscles of the neck of a wolf are well known to be so powerful that they enable the animal to carry off a sheep with ease . . .

Long sharp *tusks*? Ye Gods! Then, a little later in the book when Wolfe, his two-legged and tusk-less hero, loses patience with some hapless wretch:
The ferocious Wolfe could stand this no longer. His eyes flashed fire . . .

Sound familiar? Yet it is to this man that history has turned, uncritical and unquestioning, for the very words that have become the epitaph of the wolf in Scotland. When you read those words in the relative academic calm of Harting's book they simply strike you as ludicrous. But if Harting had read Lauder's account of the last wolf in full, you like to think he might have recognised whose influence was guiding the writing hand of the author and dismissed it as the witterings of the Wizard's disciple, a poor imitation of the Great Unknown.

Curiously, it is nothing more than an aside in Lauder's otherwise more or less factual account of the floods. As the floodwaters poured down the Findhorn laying waste to the lands around what had been MacQueen's domain, there is a pause in Lauder's narrative. He summons the shade of Sir Walter to his cause, and goes into wolf-overdrive. Incidentally MacQueen is described as a laird rather than a stalker, and Ballachrochin (Harting's Pall-a-chrocain) becomes Pollochock. Now, fasten your seatbelts:

Immediately within the pass, and on the right bank, stand the bare ruins of the interesting little mansion house of Pollochock. Macqueen, the laird of this little property, is said to have been nearer seven than six feet high, proportionately built, and active as a roebuck. Though he was alive within half a century, it is said that in his youth he killed the last wolf that infested this district. The prevailing story is this:

A poor woman, crossing the mountains with two children, was assailed by the wolf, and the infants devoured, and she escaped with difficulty to Moy Hall. The chief of Mackintosh no sooner heard of the tragic fate of the babes, than, moved by pity and rage he despatched orders to his clan and vassals to assemble at 12 o'clock to proceed in a body to destroy the wolf. Pollochock was one of those vassals, and being then in the vigour of youth, and possessed of gigantic strength and determined courage, his appearance was eagerly looked for to take a lead in the enterprise. But the hour came, and all were assembled except him to whom they most trusted. Unwilling to go without him the impatient chief fretted and fumed through the hall; till at length, about an hour after the appointed time, in stalked Pollochock dressed in his full Highland attire; 'I am little used to wait thus for any man,' exclaimed the chafed chieftain, 'and less still for thee, Pollochock, especially when such a game is afoot as we are boune after!' 'What sort o' game are ye after, Mackintosh?' said Pollochock simply and not quite understanding his allusion. 'The wolf, sir,' replied Mackintosh; 'did not my messenger instruct you?' 'Ou aye, that's true,' answered Pollochock, with a good-humoured smile; 'troth I had forgotten. But an that be a',' continued he, groping with his right hand among the ample folds of his plaid, 'there's the wolf's head!' Exclamations of astonishment and admiration burst from the chief and clansmen as he held out the grim and bloody head of the monster at arm's length, for the gratification of those who crowded around him.

'As I came through the slochk by east the hill there,' said he, as if talking of some everyday occurrence, 'I foregathered wi' the beast. My long dog there turned him. I buckled wi' him, and dirkit him, and syne whuttled his craig, and brought awa' his countenance for fear he might come alive again, for they are very precarious creatures.'

'My noble Pollochcock!' cried the chief in ecstasy; 'the deed was worthy of thee! In memorial of thy hardihood, I here bestow upon thee Seannachan, to yield meal for thy good greyhound in all time coming.'

Seannachan, or the old field, is directly opposite to Pollochock. The ten acres of which it consisted were entirely destroyed by the flood ...

Sir Thomas Dick Lauder would go on to become one of the most active members of the Scott Monument Committee that eventually heaved that colossal stone monstrosity into the airspace above Princes Street Gardens in Edinburgh. His novels are now as extinct as Scotland's wolves and much less likely to be reintroduced. Infestations of Scott are still widespread.

So where does that leave Scotland's last wolf? Lauder acknowledged in a footnote:

Wolves are believed to have been extirpated in Scotland about the year 1680, but there is reason to suppose that they partially existed in remote districts considerably after that period.

There, at least, is a rare outbreak of common sense. The last wolf known to have been killed by a man will most certainly not have been the last wolf. Everywhere in the world where wolves still occur naturally, people who live close to them speak of how difficult it is to see them. My Norwegian friends spent eight years making a half-hour film because they wanted to film only wild wolves being wild, wolves they found only by tracking them with their eyes and ears. Time after time they waited for hours, days, knowing there were wolves in the area, hearing them, tracking them, and not seeing them. Although this made their job much more difficult, it was a quality they admired. And the copious American literature of wolves is replete with similar responses among many native tribes. Lopez wrote in *Of Wolves and Men*:

Wolves are elusive, secretive creatures. L. David Mech, who has been studying them in the wild for twenty years, has come upon only a dozen on the ground that he didn't first see from an airplane or track down with the aid of a radio collar. Elusiveness is a defensive trait and it is conceivable that its function is to avoid detection by other wolves, so adjacent packs can overlap their territories and run little risk of fatally encountering each other. This would allow an area to 'breathe' more easily as game populations fluctuated. It would also facilitate the movement of dispersing wolves.

And in places like Highland Scotland in the seventeenth and eighteenth centuries, it would be a first line of defence against the two-legged creature that had brought it to the brink of extinction. It is possible too that under such circumstances wolves might refine that capacity for elusiveness by reducing their dependence on howling, adding silence to their ability to move through the land with the stealth of shadows.

The story of the Findhorn wolf and the date of 1743 have proved stubbornly durable. The efforts of the Scott-obsessed Lauder, the myth-making Sobieski-Stuarts, and Professor Harting have forged not just a nineteenth-century fairy tale but a twenty-first-century stumbling block that denies access to the truth about the wolf in Scotland. As recently as the last quarter of the twentieth century, some serious conservation voices were still lending it their support. Even David Stephen, a naturalist of uncompromising daring, wrote:

When and where was the last Scottish wolf killed? The story that ought to be true, and may well be, is that told of Macqueen of Pall-a-Chrocain, on the Findhorn, stalker to the Mackintosh of Mackintosh. Macqueen is usually given the credit for slaying the last wolf in Caledonia which, at that time, was not so stern or wild as man has since made it. The year was 1743 – a bare two years before the last of the Stuarts raised his standard at Glenfinnan.

When the black beast, as the wolf was called, had killed two children, the Laird of Mackintosh called a *tainchel* to round him up, and Macqueen was the leader of the expedition sent against him. Macqueen's story is surely the shortest and most remarkable story in the literature . . .

There follows, uncritically, the famous Lauder quotation. So David Stephen also swallowed the Harting version of events.

Then there is Erik Zimen, indisputably among the leading authorities on the wolf in Europe, but who is still willing to quote the date:

As in England, hunting alone failed to exterminate the wolf in Scotland. Forests had to be cleared before it grew rarer in the middle of the seventeenth century. The last wolf was not killed till a century later, apparently in 1743.

Pure Harting again. Yet, I can't imagine he read Harting (more likely he accepted the much repeated date and slipped in the gentle qualification of the word 'apparently'). If he had, he would surely have scoffed at the reference to the 'large black beast', because a simple reference in his book, *The Wolf,* puts the last nail in the coffin of the Findhorn story. He wrote:

Wolves in human clothing are to be seen hanging from gallows in medieval illustrations. Obviously no real distinction was made between wolves and wolf men, and presumably many of the reported

attacks on human beings were attributed to werewolves. In many of these illustrations the wolves
are black, though there are no black wolves in
Europe.

No. There are no black wolves in Europe, and the
Findhorn story is a lie.

Zimen adds a telling afterthought. In the early
1970s he led a World Wildlife Fund study of wolves in
the Abruzzi region of Italy, remarkably close to Rome.
Writing of the black wolf illustrations he noted:

> Presumably they were confused with dogs, which
> does not seem at all improbable after our experi-
> ences in the Abruzzi. During our last summer there,
> for instance, we were told a dead wolf had been
> found near Campo di Giove. We went there, and
> it was immediately obvious that it was a perfectly
> ordinary dog, though it had the colouring of a
> wolf. But we completely failed to persuade the
> many curious villagers who came to see it of the
> fact. They were convinced it was a wolf – in an area
> where men and wolves had lived side by side for
> thousands of years.

People have sought to blacken the character of
the wolf for a thousand years, perhaps longer, and
it is beyond dispute that either by accident or design
wolves were blamed for the crimes of dogs, and they
still are.

When might we have lost the last of our wolves?
Probably later than we think, for the last scattered

remnants of the wolf population would have been almost impossible to find if they chose not to be found. I have a preference for a notion that the last wolf of all died old and alone in a cave, somewhere like Rannoch Moor, far from the gaze of humankind.

CHAPTER 7
Rannoch

There is another, far less obvious, kind of com-
munication wolves employ, which is perhaps
extrasensory, or at least beyond our range of
perception. I have noticed that captive ani-
mals at rest seem to pick up cues from each
other even though there is no audible sound
and they are out of visual contact. Their backs
may be turned to each other or one may be
off in some trees in a corner of the pen. When
an animal stares intently at something, for
example, it apparently creates some kind of
tension. Other animals respond by lifting
their heads and turning without hesitation
to look at the area where the first animal is
staring. In my experience it was often the sub-
ordinate animals that responded first and the
alpha animals last. Perhaps further research
will establish a firmer foundation for this. It
hints, of course, at much.

– Barry Lopez, *Of Wolves and Men* (1978)

WOLVES ALSO DREAM. You will know of course
that they howl, and that by howling they advertise their
presence, status, numbers, location, state of health, state
of mind, purpose, and other secrecies known only to

wolves and those other tribes of nature that have good cause to listen and understand. They also yap to each other and whuff and growl intimately to mates and siblings and strangers. A domestic dog's race memory echoes some of those traits, but when a dog dreams the memory and the meaning of the dream stay within the skull. It is not so with wolves. A wolf dreams with purpose, to create a picture, a mental image important to the dreamer and therefore to all wolves. For unlike your dog, which is loyal only to you, the wolf's loyalty is to the tribe, not to the race memory but to the living race.

So the dreamer wolf sends that which was dreamed and all wolves within its reach receive it, stand still and consider its meaning, and respond in ways the dreamer will understand, dreaming and sending individually and collectively, according to circumstances and the capabilities of the dreamers, for not all wolves are equally gifted dreamers. There may be many responses to a dream in a land of wolf plenty, although unanimity in a pack is sometimes articulated in a single dream utterance. Or a failure of response is a death knell.

Dreams travel by the wolf wind. By that wind wolves can air their dreams to sow among all the wolves within reach of their dreaming. And by that wind wolves can dream back in response, for the wind works both ways, to and fro between dreamers:

– Yes, it is so.
– No, your fear is misplaced; it is not so in the west.
– Yes, this was foretold.
– No, this is news.
– I am going south.

– No, come north, the south is no longer safe.
– Deer are poor in the east. The forest is thinning.
– The wolf wind is faint. The distance between wolves is too great. Come closer.

Even in a land where wolves have been driven out, the wolf wind still blows, scenting among cold spoors for the sense of them even among their absences.

Such a land is Rannoch Moor in the Central Highlands of Scotland, straddling the borders of the old counties of Perthshire, Argyll, and Inverness-shire. In the hey-day of the Highland clans it was the last refuge of the Broken Men who survived or tried and failed to survive there in isolation, without clan lands, without a chief. There they were more or less safe from their enemies, and had only each other and the wilderness of the Moor to worry about. For similar reasons, Rannoch was also the inevitable last refuge of the Highland wolf, not the Findhorn, or Sutherland or Skye or Stirling or Killiecrankie or any one of a dozen other 'last wolf' claimants. Rannoch is, according to Fraser Darling,

the site of a great reservoir of ice in glacial times, fed by the glaciers streaming from the ice caps on the Black Mount and the other massifs. The ice piling up in the spacious saucer overspilled eastwards along the line of Lochs Rannoch, Dunalastair and Tummel, westwards through Glen Etive and Glencoe and southwards through Glen Orchy. Moor of Rannoch ice also streamed northwards into the heart of Badenoch through the long glen now filled by the narrow finger of Loch Ericht. The paths of the ice are marked by belts of moraines and the courses of streams laid down in glacial times ... On the moraines, trees followed the ice and the Moor may have been extensively wooded as recently as Roman times. Surviving fragments of this old forest can still be seen in the Black Wood of Rannoch ... in the blanket bogs for which the Moor is famous, there are the roots of the ancient forest embedded in the peat ... The Moor is but a stage in the pageant of the ages of ice, forest and mankind.

And wolf. Throughout all the stages of the pageant, there was the wolf. Rannoch Moor is the heart of the landscape of the Central Highlands, a source of lifeblood. It was the wolf's heartland too. Before and after the ice, before, during and after the trees, and long before mankind, the wolf knew that heartland as a sanctuary. And when in time things fared less well for the wolf, and the clans of Scotland for that matter, men learned from its loyalty to the Moor as a last resort, and the lost tribes – the Broken Men – adopted it as their own last resort too.

CHAPTER 8
Devon

A savage aspect, a frightful howl, an insupportable odour, fierce habits, and a malignant disposition, are the leading quali ties in its nature, which render it dangerous and detested when living and useless when dead. For this reason, hunting the wolf is a favourite diversion among the great in some countries; and it is a species of the chase at which reason need not blush, nor humanity drop a tear.

– Children's textbook, England, 1806

I PAUSED THE CD, fast-reversed it about half a minute and pressed 'play' again. This is the bit I was trying to find. I heard the quietly reassuring voice of Shaun Ellis:

'I decided the alpha male and I were going to have a fight over a duck.'

My own voice cut in at once; I heard its incredulous edge:

'*You* decided?'

'I know what you're going to say: Why on earth would I pick a fight with a dominant 120lb alpha male wolf over a duck? Have a cup of tea and a biscuit in the café and let him have it!

'But this comes back to what we call "daily testing" ... our ability to test our peers if you like, and their ability to defend us often comes down to food defence. The principle behind it is ... if he's not prepared to defend his duck in this case then we have to think seriously about his ability to defend us as a unit.

'On this occasion he was no more prepared to give up his duck than he was his leadership. And he proved this by running over to me as I picked the duck up, knocked me to the ground with his chest, then, bless his heart, he decided he would discipline me in exactly the same way he would another wolf. He decided to give me a muzzling ...'

A muzzling?

Well, bless his heart, the dominant wolf places his mouth round the muzzle of a lower ranking member of the pack. Shaun Ellis, although unquestionably a human being, believes he has achieved a middle-ranking status in a captive wolf pack, but clearly, being a human being, he has no muzzle, so the alpha male's open mouth was 'placed' round his face.

'They nip with a degree of severity they think that animal requires, so they can be quite balanced in their teaching. He had the capability to do me a serious amount of damage, but that's where the balance comes in. Even if I pinch skin here now, you can see that it leaves a mark, but I came out of that enclosure without a mark on my face.'

I heard my own voice say 'Really?' and I can imagine the expression on my face as I spoke. Shaun Ellis, who has doubtless heard that 'really?' and seen that expression a hundred times before, asked me to imagine I had

a handful of small twigs in my hands and I was start-
ing to try and crush them, and just at the point where
I think they are about to break, the grip is released.
That's what the muzzling was like.

'So they can be *that* aware in their teaching,' he said.

He analysed the moment thus:

'He obviously sensed an element of fear in me, as
you can imagine with something like that happening
for the first time; so when it was all over he came over
to me, rubbed his head against me, then it was the lick-
ing of the face and we were all bonded together in a
few short seconds to make sure we are still a family.
And to this day, if anything happened in that enclosure,
he'll still be the one I'll always run to because I know
the same balance he showed me that day instilled trust
in me to know that he will defend me at all costs.'

I asked:

'And he got to keep the duck?'

'He got to keep the duck, oh yeah,' – then a chuckle
– 'and all the others after that.'

I pressed the pause button on the CD player again.

Shaun Ellis's business card says 'Wolf Pack Management'. I met him in 2003 when I was making two
programmes for BBC Radio 4 with the collective title
of *The Real Wolf*. I have the two programmes on that
CD. Since then he has become something of a celebrity
thanks to three television programmes and attendant
publicity, an exposure to the limelight that was, alas,
shaped by the editorial values of Channel Five. I, for
one, could have wished for a more thoughtful approach
on his behalf, and for that matter on behalf of wolves.

Whatever you think of Shaun Ellis and his lifestyle as a member of a captive wolf pack, he is never less than thoughtful about his work. He is big and burly and hairy, which I suppose is what you might expect of someone with that business card and that lifestyle, but he is also as calm as he is thoughtful, and quietly spoken and not without charm, which isn't what you might expect from someone the tabloids have got in the habit of calling the Wolf Man.

Combe Martin Wildlife and Dinosaur Park is on the north coast of Devon not far from Ilfracombe, a corner of England's deep south that seems to spend much of its time catering for the kind of knotted-hanky tourism I had rather assumed was extinct. At any rate, it is in that unlikely context that I have come closest to a living wolf. It dashed behind me, about three yards from where I was sitting, doubtless wondering, as indeed I was myself, why I was inside its enclosure. There was a surreal aspect to it all, for Shaun Ellis's wolf enclosure is not only a very serious study of wolf behaviour, it is also a tourist attraction where conversation is occasionally and ludicrously drowned out by the hysterical soundtrack of screaming monkeys and belching fake dinosaurs, to name but two of the wolves' more incongruous neighbours.

The daily wolf walk is a crowd-pleaser. It is very easy to miss the profoundly serious nature of this endeavour; it would be very easy to scoff, and many find scoffing irresistible. As his girlfriend Helen would tell Channel Five while she was being groomed for a role within the pack as a nanny to imminent cubs: 'People think of me as a bit unhinged.'

But the wildlife and dinosaur park happens to be where Shaun Ellis found the land he needed. And no matter that Devon is also home to the Wolf River and a claim to the site of the killing of the last wolf in England (of which more later), his project is rooted a few thousand miles further west, in the tribal lands of the Nez Perce Indians in the northern United States. It was to the Nez Perces, you may remember, that the architects of the Yellowstone wolf reintroduction programme turned, knowing their special relationship with wolves, their fellow feeling as a hounded species,* and it was the Nez Perces who agreed to the reintroduction of the wolves on their lands when the state authorities deemed it too politically combustible to endorse. And Shaun Ellis went to meet them.

Like all people who have lived alongside wolves for thousands of years, they have their wolf stories, many of which have legendary aspects, but the nature of the legends reveals a people who thought of the wolf as a friend and a teacher, and the contrast with the wolf of Europe could hardly be more marked. The story that impressed Shaun Ellis most, the one that underpins his work in Devon, is the one in which wolves taught tribesmen the wolf talk.

It concerned the time towards the end of the American Civil War, when both conditions for the Nez Perces and the climate were extremely harsh. Tribesmen who went out on solitary expeditions were caught in storms

---

*For the definitive, full-blooded account of the way the Nez Perces were treated by the U.S. government, read Dee Brown's classic of the American West, *Bury My Heart at Wounded Knee.*

and took refuge in caves, only to discover that the caves were already occupied by wolf cubs. But instead of the frenzied hostility that greeted the Highlanders in wolf stories the adult wolves treated the Nez Perces with nothing more threatening than aloofness. There again, the tribesmen were only sheltering, not killing the cubs, and their attitude to the wolf was one of high regard, of admiration for its hunting skills and the tribe-like social organisation of the pack.

These solo treks by the Nez Perces were, according to the stories at least, serious undertakings. Holing up in a cave during the worst of winter weather was routine for them, not the inevitable life-and-death ordeal that such a story would have signified in Europe. Slowly, over time, after what Shaun Ellis described as 'a period of trust', the adult wolves would allow the tribesman to feed off the same food as they brought in for the pups. The trust improved to the point where the wolves started to teach the people how to survive the winter alongside them. Sometimes the tribesmen were away for four or five years, and when at last they returned to their villages, the chiefs said that that the language they brought back was 'the wolf talk'. Shaun Ellis took that idea at face value, wondered if there was any truth in it, and made it the foundation of his work:

'It seemed to be above anything else we could gain just by study. That's how it started many years ago. Could we go back to captive packs, get them as instinctive as possible, get them as close to nature as we can, then infiltrate the packs and live alongside them with the view to getting this language back?'

The 'language' is not a thing of recognisable human

sounds but rather a subtle blend of body posture, smell and wolf voice. But how do you persuade a wolf pack – even a captive one – with its strictly administered social hierarchy, to accept a human infiltrator and treat him as a member of the pack? Shaun Ellis's solution was inventive. He played recordings of wolf howls over loudspeakers just outside the enclosure, a phantom pack in a neighbouring territory. The result, he reasoned, would be an urge within his captive pack to boost their numbers. They couldn't do it by breeding because there was no female back then, so instead of introducing another wolf, he presented . . . himself; not as a man, certainly not as a wolf, but simply as a member of the pack, albeit one that would have to be taught the occasional lesson to reinforce the wolves' idea of his place in their scheme of things. Hence the fight over the duck, hence the muzzling, which I would imagine is as unambiguous a fragment of wolf language as any human being has ever had to learn.

And with that image firmly located in the forefront of my mind, I was invited inside the wolves' enclosure. A few years before, on Kodiak Island, Alaska, again working for radio, I had watched an adult female grizzly bear climb up from the river where she had been fishing, walk in a purposeful arc behind our small group of four, turn and walk along a path of her own making through shoulder-high fireweed, pause twenty yards away, then stand on her hind legs so that her great bear head was something like eight feet up in the air. I asked my guide, Scott Shelton, what she was doing.

'Oh she's just having a look.'

'At us?'

'Oh no, at you – she knows what I look like.'

It is a curiosity of my character for which I can take no credit, and which has astonished me more than once, that I have never felt fear in nature's company, and for the bear that was having a look at me from twenty yards away I felt only warmth and admiration. Now a wolf was ambling along a path of its making towards me from about fifty yards away and the uppermost thought in my head concerned the size of its feet. I remembered the bear then. I asked Shaun Ellis what the wolf was doing, coming for a look?

'They're already communicating with us; they're identifying you by smell, by body posture.'

Even there, even inside that high and uncompromising wire fence inside a park designed unambiguously for tourists, I felt a surge of exultation. Hey, I've been identified by a wolf!

The wolf turned back, hesitant in the face of this new creature to be identified, this creature without fear, this creature that watched and heard the rhythmic soft slap of his footfall and thrilled to something nameless, primitive and ancient. Then the monkeys started screaming again and the thing evaporated, and the creature who had to be identified by a wolf reminded himself that whatever was going on here, it was going on inside a wire fence and a wolf isn't whole as long as it is denied its natural habitat, and its natural habitat is travel within a territory of a thousand square miles, or into the unknown like Number 14 when she lost Old Blue.

I sat and watched Shaun Ellis communicating with his captive wolves, a rabbit in his hand, showing it to a wolf then running away, trying to stimulate the pre-hunting behaviour of wild wolves. As I watched I thought that while these wolves might well learn the pre-hunting behaviour from this non-wolf, they might yet never learn to hunt for themselves.

He crouched down and turned sideways-on to one wolf, inviting him in, using wolf language, the wolf apparently understanding. But it was all so far from his grand vision, which he described as 'a British Yellowstone, somewhere in the Scottish Highlands'. The theory is that you teach a captive wolf to behave like a wild wolf; then, by learning the lost wolf language, the wolf becomes the teacher and you the pupil. Then, as time goes by, wolves born in Devon with skills learned from their parents already ingrained in them, take their place in a showpiece reintroduction scheme.

There are two snags. One is, he freely acknowledges, it may well not happen in his lifetime, in which case, you have to wonder if it will happen at all, at least as he envisages it. He is, to say the least, a bit of a one-off. The other is that there is a limit to the number of wolves the enclosure can handle, and if there is to be an alpha female, and if she breeds successfully, the wolf pack needs lower-ranking females too, to act as nannies to the pups, for that is a role fulfilled by female wolves in a wild pack . . . unless of course he finds a female kindred spirit – a human one – willing to be insinuated into the pack to become that lower-ranking nanny.

At this point, almost six years after my trip to Devon, I am struggling with the philosophy of the project. Is it extraordinarily visionary, or is it grotesque, self-indulgent madness? And then, even as I was writing this, Channel Five showed two TV programmes called *Mr and Mrs Wolf*. Shaun Ellis had found Helen Jeffs, and she had given up her house and her job as a pre-school nurse and moved in with him. He was about to try to persuade her to become a wolf cub nanny in nine weeks.

'She can learn the female aspect of the wolves, and I find that very difficult,' Shaun Ellis told the cameras. By now, there were seven wolves in the enclosure, the alpha male, two other adult males, three troublesome juvenile males, and Cheyenne, a female, who had mated with the alpha male. If the mating was successful, there would be pups in nine weeks. Cue a will-she-won't-she cliffhanger at the end of programme one, by which time we have already seen Helen Jeffs faking regurgitation of food for Cheyenne in response to Shaun Ellis's instruction, 'Get her to nip around your lips', and tearfully participating in the rescue of a camerawoman from a hide inside the enclosure which the wolves had discovered. Meanwhile the never-less-than-scary sounding voice-over proclaimed, 'Helen has gone from a human nursery nurse to an apprentice wolf nanny regurgitating offal in three weeks.' At which point I felt like regurgitating my dinner over the television.

Shaun, meanwhile, had come off second best in a spat with one of the males. His role in the pack is to defuse the tensions, to break up the fights, and it seems, to lose some of them. So the camera lingers on him looking morose and nursing a couple of cuts on his face. You can almost hear the director urging him to look cowed and miserable, yet from what I remember of our interview he was philosophical about rough-and-tumble injuries, of which there must inevitably be many when you put yourself on the line as the peacemaker among three or four quarrelling wolves. I was not at all sure I was ready for part two of *Mr and Mrs Wolf*.

I can't help wondering if they would have been watching *Mr and Mrs Wolf* in that cottage in the tiny Devon hamlet of Wolverston on the River Wolf, where I knocked on the door and told a delightful old woman that I was from the BBC, making a radio programme about wolves, and I understood that this was where the last wolf in England was killed.

'That's what they say,' she said.

'Do you know anything about the story?'

'No, but my husband might. He's down the workshop. I'll call him.'

Her husband slid out from under a tractor and began talking at once, as if a visit from the BBC was an everyday occurrence. He told us what he knew, and my producer and I looked at each other, and I asked a couple of more questions and the old man spoke in response to the questions, and I looked at my producer again and detected an imperceptible shake of the head. We made our politest excuses and left. Grant Sonnex, the producer, lives near Bristol which is not a million miles away, and I was hoping against hope that he had understood the old boy, for my unattuned ears hadn't understood one word in ten.

We played it back, and in truth, we couldn't use a word of it, other than to let him begin talking and then to fade his voice under my voiceover. It was a delicious accent, and I would love to have had the time to unravel it, but it was thicker than a jar of clover honey, and as impenetrable as Flemish. If it had been television we could have used subtitles. We gleaned this: tradition said England's last wolf died nearby, in a valley bottom below Wolverton Moor where the Wolf River runs. Was it killed? Probably. Do you know when? Or how? No, no. But that's what they say. This was my first encounter with the twilight world that is the last resting place of the last wolf. I would re-enter it again and again, finally about 700 miles further north on the Findhorn River. Only the accent would change.

We had a folklorist, Jennifer Westwood, for company as we navigated the baffling, beautiful, mazy, hedged-in lanes of the valley of the Wolf River, an utterly different Devon from Ilfracombe and Combe Martin; but it was like looking for the secret of a magic spell inside a web, and this particular last wolf had had 500 years to cover its tracks. Harting's assessment of the available evidence concluded:

> 1485–1509. Some time between these two dates, during the reign of Henry VII, it is probable that the wolf became finally extirpated in England.

He doesn't mention Devon, yet if you wanted a peg to hang a theory on, surely the Wolf River is as promising as 500-year-old clues come. In Highland Scotland, for example, river names are often the oldest in the landscape. Jennifer Westwood counselled caution. It was hard, she said, to say for certain that the river was named after the killing. 'I may be unduly suspicious, but sometimes rivers are renamed.'

We followed directions from the couple in the cottage up to an ever-so-slightly eerie tree-shrouded crossroads. The name on the signpost announced Wolverston, followed by the symbol of a cross. What more do you need – Wolverston Cross, the Crossroads of the Wolf Village, right? Or is that a dangerous assumption? I asked the expert.

'Not so much dangerous as disappointing, as often as not. If this name is anything like the name Wallerton in various parts of the country . . . when you break that down the Medieval forms sound as if they've got the wolf word in it . . . but when you really look at the legal documents, it turns out to be people's names.'

So maybe Mr and Mrs Wolf lived here.

Strange how this most reviled of creatures across much of Europe from the Middle Ages onwards was also the name of choice for so many kings, warriors, would-be kings and would-be warriors. There were among England's Anglo-Saxon Kings an Ethelwulf (the Noble Wolf); a Berthwulf (the Illustrious Wolf); Eadwulf (the Prosperous Wolf); Ealdwulf (the Old Wolf) . . . but never a hint of a Child-Slaying Wolf or a Sheep-Devouring Wolf or a Black Wolf or a Long-Tusked Wolf. So although the handed-down reputation of the wolf was so unremittingly slanderous, the many qualities of the true wolf were not lost on warrior-kings.

There is a further implication: if you wanted to command the loyalty of your subjects, why choose the name of a creature that legend would have us believe was universally reviled? Could it be that there were many parts of the country, many parts of Europe, where the wolf was admired by those who lived alongside it, for exactly those qualities that appealed to a dynasty of kings, and for that matter, that appealed and still does appeal to thousands of years of generations of North American Indians and Eskimos? Shaun Ellis may have found his inspirational sources among the Nez Perces. But if the inclinations of Anglo-Saxon kings had survived the welter of history-warping storytellers and myth-makers, he might have found role models much nearer to home too.

Jennifer Westwood and I were rummaging among the possibilities of wolf names on the map while we walked a stretch of narrow road between Wolverston Cross and the high edge of Wolverston Moor. We bumped into a local woman walking a posse of dogs and asked her what she knew. Oh, she knew the story, of course, but not the detail. There was an old man in the village who knew more, but he died. But if we were to walk out onto the high moor, we'd be overlooking the spot where the deed was done, England's last wolf slain. And with a final, parting shrug she added:

'That's what they say.'

But you never find out who 'they' were, nor when they said it.

The panorama from the edge of the moor was far-flung and lovely, and the river was far below, and the maze of lanes and hedges and dark trees fused into a hidden underworld where I found it easier to believe in hobbits than wolves. I was looking for the folklorist's perspective, some unfankling of the myth-makers' knots. I listed a few of the options and put them to Jennifer Westwood:

'We're in a landscape full of wolf placenames, including the irresistible Wolf River, and perhaps the setting for one of the following:
"The last place that a wolf was seen in England."
"The last place that a wolf was seen in Devon."
"A story attached to an important local family."
"Some minor incident embroidered by local fantasy or bardic tradition."
What do you reckon?'

'As always with local tradition, it would be lovely if there were a historical basis and you thought, "here are these people who have remembered this story for such a long time,"' she said. 'But so often the folklorist's life is doomed to disappointment. Well, perhaps not disappointment exactly, but . . . it's a floating tradition. With the right kind of landscape and place names the story will attach to that place. It's eternally fascinating and eternally frustrating.'

Barry Lopez had written in *Of Wolves and Men* about his response to reading some ancient books and the attitudes to wolves they reveal.

You cannot examine any of these books without sensing that you have hardly touched in them the body of human ideas concerning the wolf. The wolf seems to move just beneath the pages of these volumes, loping along with that bicycling gait, through all human history, appraised by all sorts of men but uttering itself not a word.

And I came away from the valley of the Wolf River with the same kind of feeling. It's not the sense of the wolf that you bring away with you, but a sense of the storytellers, huddled round a winter fire, swilling fire-water cider, making mischief with a beast of which they know nothing, nothing beyond the old stories they heard from their parents, their grandparents, wisps from the mists of time. They have their whisky-drinking counterparts too in far Strathglass, with their particular local invention of the stalwart hunter hanging onto the tail of the enraged she-wolf hell-bent on ripping the throat from the cub-slaying hunter inside her den; in Waternish on Skye, in the strath of the Findhorn River where a hunter built suspiciously like Scotland's most durable warrior hero single-handedly killed the huge black wolf that had devoured two children as they crossed the winter hills with their mother. But alas for the storytellers, there were no black wolves in Europe.

Mr and Mrs Wolf part two lived up to all my forebodings. Two hours of thoughtful prime-time television devoted to wolves could have made inroads into centuries-old prejudice. But two hours of tabloid prime-time television that preyed on its perception of the sensibilities of a Channel Five audience, replete with subliminal graphics of wolf teeth in close-up on a blood-red background, might just have set back by decades the cause of public approval of wolf reintroduction. Even now, even in the twenty-first century while wolves are steadily reclaiming old haunts in western Europe, while the European Union's Species and Habitats Directive prods its member governments into recognition of their responsibilities in the matter of restoring indigenous wildlife species where they have been lost, while Yellowstone's reintroduction programme blazes a trail of enlightenment whose benefits are so self-evident and so well documented that they dazzle with potential . . . even as that kind of headway is being made on both sides of the Atlantic, British television's contribution is *Mr and Mrs Wolf*, two programmes not about wolves at all, but about a couple filmed in such a way as to leave an impression of two eccentric people doing something absurdly dangerous in the company of ferocious creatures. Every wolf stereotype was dropped in, not by Shaun Ellis and Helen Jeffs, but by the programme's anonymous voice-over. Oh, the female wolf Cheyenne had her pups (a difficult birth in which the fifth pup became stuck in her birth canal, so that a vet had to be brought in, she had to be darted with a gun, operated on, and paraded in front of the cameras again still suffering from the after-effects of the ordeal and the anaesthetic) and she did eventually bring them out to the two human pack members, and there is no denying that was extraordinarily affecting, and Shaun Ellis told the camera: 'We've all just been witness to the miracle that is the wolf.'

No. The miracle that is the wolf is elsewhere, living on the move, ranging over hundreds of square miles, doing nature's bidding, mixing it with bears, lynx, elk, eagle, and the other fellow-travellers of a northern wilderness, shaping the very ecosystem in which it lives, feeding thousands of mouths, creating opportunities for dozens of other species of mammals, birds, insects, plants, and making people aware of the debt we owe to nature in that far wolf country where people and wolves and wilderness still rub shoulders, and where nature makes the rules of engagement. For centuries we have taken from nature, and for the first time in our own evolution we are aware of the worth of conservation and we have all the information we need to restore much of that which we have taken. The wolf is the supreme agent to effect that kind of change. That is the miracle that is the wolf.

Shaun Ellis said in the first of the two programmes, 'To help and understand a creature you have to walk the same path.'

Yes, but that is no wolf path his programmes walked.

He also urged his girlfriend: 'Don't think like a human – think like a wolf.'

But that is simply impossible. A wolf thinks like a wolf every minute of every day and night. The human mind can learn something of wolf behaviour and think that it understands why a wolf behaves in a particular way in particular circumstances, but it is a human appreciation of what the wolf thinks, not a wolf's appreciation. The very instruction, 'Don't think like a human, think like a wolf,' is a human thought. And the moment the two human beings start talking to each other again, they cease thinking the way they think wolves think. The wolf never stops thinking like a wolf.

In my own work with swans, which includes watching the same Highland mute swan territory over thirty years, I convinced myself of only one thing with absolute certainty – that I do not think like a swan. And if you did ever learn to think like a wolf, you would not limit it with a fence, for that is the opposite of the way a wolf thinks, nor would you impose on the pack an alien species, for it makes no more biological sense to ask a wolf to interact with a human being as a member of its pack than with an elephant, a kangaroo, a troupe of screaming monkeys or a fake dinosaur.

And yet Shaun Ellis has something remarkable to offer as an evangelist for the wolf. It is undeniable that he has gained insights that could prove invaluable in a genuine wolf reintroduction programme. There again, a genuine wolf reintroduction programme would not involve captive wolves but wild ones brought in from European landscapes similar to our own, landscapes where the wolf's principal prey is deer, for it is by manipulating the deer herds that the wild wolf can begin to transform bare Highland glens and restore to them the diversity of life that belongs there. But if I had something to do with such a project, I would like to have someone on my team who could speak the lost wolf language.

CHAPTER 9
The Black Wood

TREES REMEMBER WOLVES. The oldest pines, the three-and-four-hundred-year-olds, know the brush of wolf fur, the soft, deep slap of their footfall on the forest floor. They hand down the sense of wolves to the wolfless generations of young trees, and these grow older remembering the sense of wolves so that they are ready for the wolves' return, which they know to be inevitable. The oldest tree in the Black Wood of Rannoch is a Scots pine of massive dark strength. When its seed was sown (a casual conspiracy of parent tree and crossbill and wind) it was a tree among many trees. Rannoch Moor undulates to far mountain walls at every compass point, an inland sea that breaks on mountain shores, but a sea of rock and heather and lochans and peat, of red deer and red foxes, of wildcats, of grey crows and golden eagles, of summer skylarks and winter swans, of wind-weary grass and the buried bones of dead trees. Once it was wooded from shore to shore. The Black Wood survives along the south shore of the moor. The old trees still remember the touch of wolf skin on tree skin, still long for it. Nothing else still living in the country of Rannoch has that memory.

Beneath the oldest tree, the land is hollow. There is a difficult way in among rocks to a small cave whose entrance is hidden. It is roofed and buttressed by the tree's roots, walled by rock, floored by cool, dry earth. The tree's grandmother was young – perhaps 50 years old – when a singular wolf first appeared there. She came down to the cave on a pale-green, stone-still morning of late April. She had been travelling all night, encouraged by a full moon. Just like the people, she marked time by the place of the sun and the stars in her sky, by the shape and brightness of the moon. The roundest moon was the best for hunting and travelling, the blackest, moonless, starless night was the worst, but sometimes better than daylight.

The people made a story: the wolf howls at the moon. No. The wolf is most active under the full moon because it assists travelling. And it howls most when it is most active. But it never howls when it hunts. And it has no reason to howl at the moon.

See her face in the rocks! Ah, but you can't, can you? What you need to see her face in the rocks is a race memory you can tap into that spans hundreds of years. Wolves have the required memory, for they move in the ageless pageant of all wolves. And the tree has known the face in the rocks all its life, knows it for what it is, because trees remember wolves.

Her face? Well, her eyes are pale gold, and small for the size of the face, and set in jet black ovals that thicken towards their inner edges and leak a jet black tear on each side of the muzzle. Each eye is also set in a wider circle of tan and dark grey fur and these reach up into her forehead which is mostly black but defined below her ears with a narrow echo of the same tan. Her ears are short and erect and forward-facing and rimmed in black, and the short fur there is tan and grey and white, and black again at the centre. Her muzzle is the deepest shade of tan on top, but abruptly white and pale grey on the sides and round her mouth. Her nose is small and black. She wears a ruff of bright white rimmed with dark grey and black and tan. If you could see her you might think her face beautiful.

So she came down through the rocks and she was sure of her way, guided by the discernible path worn by uncounted years of wolves. She was not led there nor was she pointed there, and she had never been there before, but she knew at once that it was a wolf place. And a wolf place does not stop being a wolf place just because the land runs out of wolves. For there is no such thing as the last wolf, no end to the pageant of wolves.

She had the knowledge to find the way without faltering. The place had not changed, not stopped being suitable. She saw the face in the rocks that welcomed her: this is your place for as long as you need it. The face is Nature in the guise of Wolf. It is her own face and it is the face of all the wolves of the pageant.

She came alone. She had travelled alone constantly for a year, but unlike many lone wolves she did not choose solitude. Rather she had survived alone the killing of her pack in Strathspey, far to the north-east of Rannoch Moor. She had a lowly status in a pack of seven. The lower-ranking pack members are often acutely resourceful because they enjoy none of the privileges of rank and eke out their livings from scraps and leftovers and a talent for compromise. When the hunters began killing, the pack had scattered, but six of the seven were tracked down relentlessly. She survived, not by running but by lying on the bed of a shallow river, submerged all bar the tip of her nose. The water masked her scent and she was the colour and stillness of rocks. The hunting hounds did not have her knowledge. No wolf taught her to lie that way, but the knowledge was in her.

Since then she had followed a ragged route southwest, searching for other wolves. She had found none. The old wolf places she knew were cold. Wherever she crossed or followed the paths of her ancestors she sensed only their absence. Finally she reached the northernmost edge of the Moor of Rannoch, and although she had never seen it before, she knew what it was, that hope lay out there among the rocky, peaty, watery, heathery waves of that moorland sea. She crossed it easily in a night, and came in among the first trees of the Black Wood. She homed in on a solitary pine tree and saw at last the dark hint of the hollow beneath. She sidled deftly between two rocks, then leapt over a blockage – a third rock – and found the entrance. The chamber beyond smelled cool and dry and woody. She paused and scented everything near and far. In the chamber there had been no wolf, no fox, no wildcat for a long time. She stepped at last deep into its shadow, made a tight furred curve of herself, and pulled her tail across her muzzle. She sighed and closed her eyes on her solitude.

CHAPTER 10
Norway

THE RADIO ASSIGNMENT that had taken me to Devon then took me to Norway, where wolves had reintroduced themselves to old heartlands more than a hundred years after a sustained cull had wiped out their forebears. Norway's wolves simply walked home. A pair crossed the border from Finland into the northmost corner of Norway, rounded the northern tip of Sweden, then began the long march down through Norway to the valley of the Gluma river in the south of the country. To human eyes it is a formidable trek, the better part of a thousand miles. But travel is what a wolf does best, and wolves seeking new territories have made distance-no-object journeys forever. Now Norway is home to four packs, which is the most the Norwegian government allows. If this number were to be exceeded, I was told that they would take action to limit the number of packs to four, which is a polite way of saying they would initiate a cull, which is another polite way of saying they would start killing wolves again. But thus far, Norway has mostly been an accommodating host to its homecoming wolves.

The radio project was to pursue an idea called *The Real Wolf* (as opposed to all the other kinds that fester in the darkest recesses of historical prejudice and vested human interest all across the northern hemisphere), but somewhere in the back of my mind, the seed for this book was already sown and I was also looking for lessons – and truths – that I could bring to bear on my native land, where Scots had raised historical prejudice to an art form for the masses. And there, for much of the twenty-first-century population, it remains.

So somewhere between Amsterdam and Oslo and at around 30,000 feet, the thought occurred to me that what Scotland needed was a border with Finland, thus side-stepping the apparently overwhelming difficulties of government wolf policy (there is none) and public opinion (see above) that still fankle every prospect of a thoughtful reintroduction of the wolf to Highland Scotland. Alas for the prospect of wolves reintroducing themselves to Scotland, the land bridge with Scandinavia fell into the North Sea some time ago, and a drifting Scotland bumped into England instead, and the English disapproved of wolves even more than the Scots.

Time passes, tides turn. Scotland is reintroducing beavers, albeit with all the conviction of Canute at high tide. It may have taken 15 years of talking and false starts, but it is a beginning, and for that matter, a precedent: a mammal has been reintroduced. But while I contemplate the prospects for wolf reintroduction, ahead lie the massed ranks of politicians in Europe, London and Edinburgh, landowning intransigence, farmers large and small, mountaineers and mountain bikers and hill-runners and hillwalkers and tourists, and even some unimaginative conservationists, all worried about being eaten, or worse, being half-eaten but left alive. The wolf will return despite them all, because that tide has turned, because the wolf has begun to drift from the margins of conservation thinking towards the mainstream. But the pace of the reintroduction will not be swift. Meanwhile, I was looking for arguments and ammunition in a country where people were growing accustomed to living alongside wolves again, and at least some of them considered it a privilege.

Driving north out of Oslo, the view quickly filled with mountains and trees, naturally occurring trees that grew to something like a naturally occurring treeline. I saw my first moose since Alaska five years before, standing alone and dead-still among roadside trees, a dark ebony colour, looking like a sculpture of a moose or a caricature of itself until it turned its moose-head to follow the car's progress. The broad beauty of the Gluma kept us company.

We stayed in a farmhouse on its east bank, built in 1797, dark timber with a turf roof from which birch saplings and other self-sown plant life sprang. They shaved it every now and then, but the roots bound the roof together and helped to anchor it. There were otter and beaver prints in the riverbank mud nearby, and a pair of sandpipers in the garden. It was called Langodden, the long bend in the river, which describes its situation perfectly. It belonged to Grete and Hakon Langodden who lived next door, and who took their surname from the place where they lived. They and their son and their grand-daughter were the only four people in Norway with that name.

I warmed to them at once, warmed to their determined lifelong attachment to their place on the map. I fell in love with Norway at once and, I suspect, forever.

And somewhere out there in that endless, north-making sprawl of mountain and forest, there were wolves. I was not naïve enough to believe that I could step off a plane, wander off into the forest and watch wolves in the handful of days at my disposal, but at the very least, I wanted to come away with the *sense* of them in their landscape, a landscape to which they had returned voluntarily after a hundred years of absence. If I could see how it worked here, I could see how it might work back across the North Sea. One of the joys of occasionally working with an organisation like the BBC's Natural History Unit is the preliminary research that underpins a project like this, so that I, as the writer and presenter of the programme, arrive in the right place at the right time to meet the right people. So the door of the 200-year-old farmhouse of Langodden opened, a voice called out a greeting, and I rose from the kitchen table to meet Bjorn and Gaire.

Bjorn and Gaire were the wildlife film-makers whose wolf programme, eight years in the making, had just aired on Norwegian television. Gaire would be the source of the walking story about the naked man and the 'concert from wolves at 200 metres'. Their passion not just for wolves, but for allowing them to behave like wolves unmolested by science's determination to follow their every movement with laptops and radio collars and spotter planes, was as blatant as it was infectious, and it was vehemently declared before we had finished our first cup of coffee. It was expressed in ever-so-slightly fractured English and with good humour, so that we all laughed as much as I marvelled at the slowly unfurling life of the wild wolf.

'So,' I said, as we got ready to explore the territory of the Koppang wolf pack, 'we have an area of about 1,000 square miles of forest and mountains, right?'

'Yes.'

'Three or four wolves, right?'

'Yes.'

'And it's summer, which is the worst possible time of year to try and find them, right?

'Yes.'

'Realistically, what are our chances of getting close to wild wolves?'

'Well ... maybe if we are lucky we can have a smell.'

And we piled into Bjorn's ancient Mercedes estate car and headed for the woods, laughing. Two hours later, we pulled off the road high above a wide-bottomed valley and overlooking a small lake where the unmistakable profile – and voice – of a great northern diver cruised the steely-blue water. If there is one sound that might be said to rival the rising howl of a wolf as the totemic voice of wild northern places, it is surely the down-curving cry of the loon. That voice rose towards us and I thought I heard wolf kinship there. Bjorn was saying that of all the packs in Scandinavia and all their territories, this was the place with the best chance of seeing wolves. But that's in winter, of course, when you can track them in the snow, when they use the rivers and the lakes as highways, when it can never get too cold for wolves, when the prey of the wolves is at its most vulnerable and grows steadily weaker as winter deepens while the wolves only grow stronger. Besides, the film-makers use many eyes. They have a network of friends and contacts all across this part of

Norway who report wolf sightings. One of them had called that morning to Bjorn's car phone with a sighting three days before. Should we go, I wondered.

'Three days – could be a hundred miles away by now.'

For all that wolves love to travel, they also have favourite places within their territory and this is one of them. We broke out the coffee and something to eat and settled to watch for a while, and Gaire, the quieter of the pair, and less confident with his English, began to paint wolf pictures:

'Two winters ago, I was watching seven wolves here. First thing I saw was a roe deer. Then I saw some other dark patches, and thought it was just places where the sun has taken the snow away. But then I saw these things begin to lie on their backs and I thought, "This is wolves." First, three wolves, then I saw four more a little further out, and it was wolf tracks in the snow all over that big area. It was . . .' he paused, searching for the right image, 'like playing a football match!'

'Liverpool versus Man U,' said Bjorn.

So I told them there was an English football team called Wolves, thinking this would be news to them.

'Oh yes,' said Bjorn. 'Wolverhampton Wanderers. They play in Division One now, I think. They were my favourites when I was a boy.'

'They play in yellow and black,' said Gaire.

It was not what I had expected to be discussing in Norway's wolf-wilderness. Gaire resumed his picture painting, complete with sound effects.

'Another time, I heard the cubs at one in the morning.'

And he demonstrated the high-pitched babbling of the cubs.

'Then the answer from the alpha male, two kilometres away.'

And as he mimicked the deep wolf voice rising then falling again in unpredictable bluesy slides and intervals, against that backdrop of the rise and fall of the valley, the lake, river, woods, clearings, fold after fold of forested hills yielding at last to 6,000-feet mountains, something danced between my shoulder blades. And suddenly the wolf was changing in my mind. The two Norwegians were beginning to show me a creature going about its everyday business, small in a huge landscape. The captive wolves in Devon, where the radio project had begun, were too large in a landscape too small. It was a head-spinning moment, and head-spinning moments had been missing in Devon.

'I heard it, then silent a long time, then it started again . . . '

I asked him what that sound meant to him. He sighed, thought about it for a few moments, then he said this:

'You sit there in the winter time, waiting, hoping that something will happen. You freeze a little. You take a little cup of tea. And you're looking. And looking. At trees full of snow. Nothing happens. Maybe you hear a little bird. And then you hear this noise. Starting very low, and you're thinking, 'Where is it? Where is it? You know? You can feel how your whole body is looking for where this wolf is. It's a very special feeling. It's the voice of the wild.'

Bjorn said: 'And it's strong, very strong-loud.'

Gaire said: 'Yes, and this voice, you bring it with you in the body, for many, many, many days.'

That silenced us all, and in that silence I wondered what he was getting at. It wasn't that I didn't understand him, it was just that I wondered where he went in his head when the voice of a wolf, which he must have heard many, many, many times, lingered deep within him these many, many, many days.

Yes, and this voice, you bring it
with you in the body
for many, many, many days.

You even try to sing its
slippery cadences;
so many, many, many ways

to hear, interpreting it
as wolf-like as you dare;
so many, many, many plays

of light illumining it,
with you in the body
for many, many, many days.

Gaire was talking again. 'Other friend, he was living on the west side of this area. He calls me one Saturday morning, Gaire, you gotta come over. He has sled dogs, these dogs had been very upset and made much noises . . . '

And so he told me the story of the naked man and the concert of wolves at 200 metres, the walking story that grew legs and made a grotesque dissonance of that concert of wolves in fourteen days. That was in fourteen days. Imagine one hundred and forty days. One hundred and forty years.

Far below us, the loon broke into our silence, a voice like a thin moan of wind; we all raised binoculars towards the sound, saw the bird swinging in slow circles the way a small boat moves on a bow anchor, and we exchanged smiles.

'It's good,' I said, 'but I'm not carrying it anywhere in the body.'

And then we were laughing and putting away our flasks and wrapping uneaten sandwiches and boarding the old Mercedes. As we drove, I decided this:

The wolf has a power. Wittingly or unwittingly – wittingly I hope, but I have no way of knowing – that power embraces the capacity to stir in other creatures an awareness of need; not the needs of wolves, but the needs of nature, the needs of the planet we call Earth. Specifically, the wolf has the power to reach *us* – the human species – although we comprise demonstrably the single most determined source of great suffering imposed on wolves, and for that matter on all nature, on planet Earth. But if there is ever to be a way for us to reconnect *as a species* with the needs of nature, if we are ever to rediscover *as a species* those fundamentals of nature that are part of our make-up too, but which we have chosen to discard, it will only be achieved by learning to listen again to nature's voice. And there is only one voice of nature with that persuasive power, one voice that you bring with you in the body for many, many, many days. We must learn to live again, I told myself, with the wolf in our midst. And then I went south to Rendal to meet a sheep-farmer called Karl.

Karl was a third-generation sheep-farmer. He was tall, strong, dignified, hospitable, eloquent and immensely likeable. And, as I soon discovered, he was also passionate about farming, about land use, and passionately against wolves. Yet as we walked around his farm, his rapport with a handful of ewes and lambs in a small field was almost childlike. It was obvious from the outset where his sympathies lay, and it was equally obvious before our conversation had progressed beyond pleasantries that he had decided I was a friend of wolves. And not once in our conversation did he raise his voice or dodge a question. He began by telling me this story:

'Two years ago we had a man working in the forest. He was surrounded by nine wolves. They went round him in a circle, nearer and nearer, threatening him. That was a *real* occasion.'

His stress on the word real was pointedly for my benefit as a friend of wolves. I asked if the man was alone.

'Yes. He was very scared, and refused to work in the forest for weeks after that. People *fear* the wolves. Almost everybody in Rendal fears the wolves. Parents have taken to driving their children to school instead of letting them walk because they fear attacks.'

He explained that the tradition in Norway had been to let sheep roam in the forests in the summer, but since the wolves returned in 1998 he had fenced his sheep all year round, until the year before I met him.

'Last year, we tried to keep the sheep in the forest and I lost more than 100 sheep out of 350.'

'Are you certain all these were killed by wolves?'

'Yes. Seventy-three were killed one night. I was there but I couldn't do anything to stop it.'

'You actually saw this happening?'

'Yes, I saw the sheep, the dead sheep, the wounded sheep which I had to shoot, to kill them myself. But I didn't see the wolves.'

'Did people come to verify that these were wolf kills?'

'Yes, they did. Of course they were killed by wolves. I have seen it so many times myself. I was quite sure.'

'How many farms have been affected round here?'

'Six farms, but earlier there were more, but they quit farming because of the wolves and the bears. They have given up. It's too hard to keep on. But I am not giving up . . .

'Because . . . ?'

'Because if we give up, this beautiful area will be just wolves and bears here. We want *people* to live here and farm and have sheep and cows. If we are to keep on farming the wolves and bears must leave or be shot.

I don't hate wolves. I don't hate any animal. But I don't like them, I don't like them near me, in my surroundings. They belong in the wilderness and there isn't enough wilderness here to keep wolves.'

I said that to someone from a small country like Scotland, Norway's tracts of mountain forest felt almost endless.

'Norway is a small country,' he said. 'We are using the forest here. We have roads, there are cottages, we are picking berries and we are hunting, and the wolves are threatening all of these activities. So we feel we don't have enough wilderness.'

'So would you rather there were no wolves in Norway at all?'

'Yes. That would be my wish.'

'Do you think that's fair on the wolves?'

'I think there is enough wilderness in Russia, in Alaska, to keep the wolves. The wolves aren't threatened from a global perspective. So I don't think we have to keep them in the little Norway.'

The little Norway's lucrative hunting industry concurs. Hunters and wolves compete for moose, among other things, and attacks by wolves on hunters' dogs are not rare. On the other hand, wolves don't kill hunters. The last 'documented' attack on a hunter in Norway was in 1800, and we have already seen how reliable such documenting of wolf behaviour was in Europe back then.

Every year, however, hunters are killed by moose, and so, indirectly are non-hunters, for moose on Norwegian roads are a regular source of road traffic accidents. But no-one wants to remove moose from the little Norway, nor do they drive their children to school rather than let them walk because moose are in the forests. The thing about a moose is that it is so useful to people; hunters love to hunt them and people love to eat them. (I'm with them there: I had a moose steak in Norway and it was sublime.) But you don't put a wolf head on your wall and you don't eat wolf steaks, and only in Alaska did I ever meet a man who owned up to using wolf fur for his mitts and to trim the hood of his parka.

And although I was impressed by the Norwegian sheep-farmer, and although it would be so easy to sympathise with the logic of his arguments, I felt there was something missing, and that something left me feeling vaguely uncomfortable. His arguments were all based solely on the interests of people. And are we really willing to tolerate wilderness only if it is populated by creatures with which people can feel comfortable? Have we strayed so far from our origins as one of nature's tribes that we cannot permit a single discordant note, a single edgy presence? No-one disputes that Norway has wilderness, but it is a restored wilderness, and it was restored by the return of the wolf. For any wilderness that has its top predator removed artificially – say by a government-sponsored cull – stops being wilderness. People can't manage wilderness, because when they try, as they have done in Scotland for the last few hundred years, they do so by putting the interests of people first.

I suggested something like that to Karl, and asked why it was not enough to be willing to share his place on the map with wolves knowing the government would compensate him for sheep killed by wolves. He said that his grandfather had farmed sheep here, his father had farmed sheep here, and he would farm sheep here. But feeding wolves was not why he raised sheep.

Twenty-four hours earlier, his fellow Norwegian Gaire had said to me:

'Yes, and this voice, you bring it with you in the body for many, many, many days,' and I had felt a kind of soaring optimism for the potential for our species to reconnect with wolves. But after talking to Karl, after thinking about him and his way of life and how he saw his own place on the map and how he perceived that it was farming that made it beautiful (and although he never used the words, the unspoken implication seemed to be that that other wolf-and-bear wilderness was a kind of ugliness), I was made uneasy. I was suddenly acutely aware of the power of the phrase 'a wolf in sheep's clothing' – it is the ultimate deceit. And I had a new definition of the word 'overkill' – 73 sheep killed by two wolves in one night.

The idea behind the radio project that had taken me to Norway in the first place, to get to grips with something called *The Real Wolf*, must surely embrace both these extremes of response to the proximity of wolves if it was to produce anything like a balanced assessment . . . but only if it was to produce anything like a balanced assessment, and I never much cared for balanced assessments or balanced writing for that matter. And mine is a nature writer's perspective, and my nature writing is informed by the fact that I am also a journalist, and the journalist in me was taught many years ago to question every shred of received wisdom that comes my way, regardless of how sincerely it may have been offered, in case it should somehow mask or diminish my own conclusions of what I perceived to be the truth.

I had come to Norway in the first place because I am fascinated by wolves, enthralled by the place they occupy in a northern hemisphere ecosystem when they are permitted to behave like wolves. And the truth about the wolf – *one* truth about the wolf – is that it can be like a bridge in all our lives, a bridge where enlightenment may cross, a bridge to a place where we don't make all the rules and where our species is not always in charge. And if some people are disadvantaged by our willingness to allow the proximity of wolves back into our lives, people like sheep farmers and hunters, then that is simply part of the price that we pay for the privilege of a closer walk with natural forces, part of the debt that we owe for all that we have taken out of nature for far too long. We cannot rationalise every decision we ever make as a species on the basis of whether or not it will be good for the economy; sometimes the greater good of planet Earth must come first, and the wolf, as the master-manipulator of northern hemisphere ecosystems, is an agent for that greater good.

We had planned a late night out on a mountaintop at the heart of the Koppang pack's territory with Bjorn. But first there was a private screening at his house of the film he and Gaire had made for Norwegian television. It was beautifully done, both understated and passionate at the same time, and its characteristic motif was a constant return to sequences of long shots, the wolves tiny in a huge landscape and travelling, always travelling. Bjorn liked these long shots too for the way they symbolised the life of a handful of wolves in a territory of a thousand square miles. He added: 'I could have got closer but then I risked to scare them.'

And there was another perspective on the relationship between people and wolves. There were the parents who decided to start driving their children to school for fear of attacks, and there was the film-maker working with wolves day after day for eight years who didn't want to get too close in case *he* scared *them*.

Bjorn cooked moose steaks, a moose he had shot himself, and, yes, there was a trophy head on the wall in his sitting room. I asked him where he had shot it. He led me out on to the veranda (Norwegians love verandas and balconies) with its miles-wide view over forests and hills, gestured at that expansive land as if the answer to my question was somewhere out there, and then the sweep of his arm ended by pointing down at the place on the veranda where he had told me to stand.

'Right here,' he grinned.

'You shot a moose from your own balcony?'

'Yes, he was standing in the edge of the trees there. Here, you don't go to the supermarket. The supermarket comes to you.'

The steak was served with mushrooms and onions and roast potatoes and it was as good as any meat I have ever eaten. Then we headed out into the northern evening for the mountain, knowing it wouldn't get dark, knowing our best ghost of a chance of the sight or the sound (I'd settle for that) of a wild wolf was up there and late in the evening. Or perhaps we would just get a smell.

The car was pounding up unmetalled forest roads when Bjorn suddenly said: 'Stop here, stop here, stop here!'

We jumped out and crouched over four huge footprints in the mud. Moose tracks are everywhere in these forests, but these were not moose. Even I knew that only one animal made tracks like that – bears. Bjorn stood up and said, 'That was very big surprise!'

He declined to explain how he had spotted them

from inside the car at 30 miles an hour. But they were old. 'This could be from the autumn,' he said.

So the wolves have bears for company. Goody.

We left the car soon after and began to climb up ever-narrowing paths through the trees, the air cooling noticeably as we climbed. We watched the path. We found wolf tracks, and although they too were old, something slid into place alongside them. It was exhilarating as a native of wolf-less Scotland to walk here, knowing that a wolf had walked this path before me, and will walk it again after me, and find my footprints there. Briefly, we have shared the same few square yards of our travelling lives. Our paths have crossed.

We were making for the summit where an old fire-watcher's cabin now served as a wolf-watcher's bothy. The forest, like all good natural forests, closed in on us, then fell back and opened up grassy clearings. It also thinned out and the stature of the trees diminished as we climbed. And sightlines expanded, opening long views to the north. There were miles and miles and miles of this stuff, and big mountains beyond.

At last we left the trees behind and half the world appeared. I looked around through 360 degrees at the sprawl of hill and forest and river valley – the mighty Gluma again. Bjorn watched me for a few moments, then said, 'Now you see almost the whole territory of the wolf pack.'

Almost. It's colossal. I have heard scaremongering 'experts' predict that if the wolf was reintroduced into Scotland, we would end up with between 300 and 400 wolves. Yet in the whole of Norway, with so much more suitable habitat and abundant prey, there are between 20 and 30 wolves, and most Norwegians simply never see them. Scotland would do well to reach 20 wolves.

Down there somewhere, in the closest 1,000 square miles, there were a handful of wolves, four of them, possibly five, travelling, always travelling. I heard Gaire's voice again: 'Where is it? Where is it? You can feel how your whole body is looking for where this wolf is.'

And I was looking with my whole body, and we all trooped off to the summit where a peregrine falcon leapt from a rock, a grey slash across the sunset. I heard Karl's voice again: 'There is no room for them in the little Norway.'

It was almost 10 p.m. Bjorn said: 'We have the sun for one more hour. I think we will sit down and just relax, maybe take a cup of coffee.'

A cup of coffee on a Norwegian mountaintop watching the sun set in the north has a lot to commend it. At any second a wolf might howl from the trees below, the sound curling up on the wind like a buzzard on a thermal, but the wind sang alone and grew cold.

I had another of those 'unsound but illuminating thoughts' (the phrase, you may remember, was Ernest Hemingway's) that punctuate my nature writing life and help the writing along, and it was this: 'There's the essence. The real wolf is *not* seen, *not* heard. It exists beyond us. It always will be beyond us. But we all carry our own picture of it with us.'

And here's mine. The quest of these two radio programmes had begun with a captive wolf almost at my feet in Devon. But here, on this Norwegian mountain-top that was a wolf pack's landmark, watching the sun vanish and the deep-blue midnight descend on the forest, I had never felt closer to wildness in my life. I have been on mountains at midnight before and slept in forests, but the difference here was the possibility of wolves, the certainty of their unseen, unheard presence. The wolf matters first and foremost for its own sake. Beyond that, it is our passport back to deeper appreciation of wildness – it is as simple as that.

We walked back down into the forest, still watchful, still hopeful.

What was that?

What *was* that? It was a sound far-off at the edge of my hearing, deep-throated and rising then lost, shredded by the wind. I turned to Bjorn.

'What was that?'

'I did not hear it.'

'It was deep, something at the edge of my hearing.'

'Perhaps it was a wolf.'

But I was unwilling to claim it. If Bjorn had heard it, that would have been different. I said: 'It was a troll.'

'It could be.'

And we walked back to the car chuckling while robins sang and cuckoos and woodcock called.

And in the car, somewhere around 2 a.m., far down the forest road, just beyond the range of the headlights, something ran across the road and vanished into trees and it was fast and pale and the last I saw of it was the flourish of a thick tail. And what was that? It could have been, we agreed. It could have been. The wolf, always moving at the edge of things, and travelling, always travelling.

My BBC producer Grant Sonnex and I spent part of our last day in Norway revisiting the Jugenhotte, the Canyon of the Trolls. Norwegians love their trolls, their troll stories, their troll dolls of every shape and size. Scotland's worst tourist-trap shops sell tartan dolls by the bucket-load; Norway's sell trolls.

We had stopped at the canyon during our first exploration of the wolf territory with Bjorn and Gaire. Grant wanted to record its teeming, echoing ravens, and I was happy to have a bit of time to gather my thoughts and make notes sitting on the canyon rim.

In simple geological terms, it was a glacier dam that burst, not that there is anything simple about the process or its protracted aftermath, but the result is a huge gouge out of the land. You stand on the rim peering down into its giddy depths, vertical rock walls sparsely colonised by ragged hedges of nimble-footed pines that first thrust out a speculative trunk into the airspace then turned at right angles and climbed towards the sun. The river was in shadow, and so far below that its voice was drowned out by ravens, the adults bringing in prey to lusty fledglings. The fledglings fluttered and screamed on the ledges, demanding more. Quite a place to take your first flight. It takes brave ravens to hatch out there where trolls and broken boulders conspire far, far below, and lie in wait of just one first false step before juvenile wings have grown articulate in the peculiar speech of mobile canyon air. The Jugenhotte was a natural amphitheatre for echoes, so that the uneasy impression was of hordes of ravens instead of just a few dozen.

A long, grey glacial slash shone across the face of the mountain, like the falcon crossing the sunset: this too is a landmark on the pack's travels. I began to wonder if their thousand square miles contained so much as a single dull acre. If it did, I didn't see it.

I raised my own voice in my imperfect impersonation of a raven, and heard it echo back to me, the echo spilled from a raven's mouth. A Canadian biologist once told me that ravens had the largest animal vocabulary after human beings. I wondered what raven meaning I had just uttered, and what the raven replied, and what the rest of the canyon made of our echoed exchange.

I spent some of the last evening on the balcony of a spotless motel room, writing in sunshine, watching swifts that nested two balconies to the south. I left the door to my balcony open all evening but no wolf howl drifted in, although a swift flew round the room in the early morning and flew out again. There are worse ways to be woken than by the flight of a swift.

The long road south was the beginning of the end of it all. The land softened, pines and birches gave way to softer trees. Eventually there were no more mountains.

Oslo airport is the only truly beautiful airport I have ever seen. Huge curved laminated wooden beams support a vast and airy space. It is clean and quiet, the staff welcoming and helpful. A huge sculpture adorns the entrance. It is of some Norse god or other, one arm outstretched, one drawn back as if to hurl some devastation or other – a missile or thunderbolt or the kind of god-rock that bursts glacier dams – except that the object in his hand is a paper aeroplane. An airport where you smile as you enter is unique in my experience of the species.

It may be that Scotland will not reintroduce wolves in my lifetime, although I think it will. But if some political deity of Edinburgh or London decrees, say, a 50-year moratorium on all mammal reintroductions because, say, a reintroduced beaver felled a listed tree in Argyll, or dammed a trout stream, then I may move to Norway.

We flew. We landed in Amsterdam. Holland was flat with straight lines. Grant and I parted company there. He flew on to London, I to Edinburgh, where the tilt of the landing aircraft restored to me the sight of a mountain skyline – Perthshire, where a small pine-lined cottage waited for me among forested hills, among forested wolf-less hills.

I picked up my rented car, and headed up the familiar M9 towards the familiar mountains. My mind was in a far forest.

What was that?

CHAPTER 11
The First Dreams

TWICE THE DREAMING. *Twice the failure of others to respond in dreaming.*

It was as she had begun to fear: in all the wolf lands of her travels since she left the high mountain plateau and pinewoods of the north-east, no wolves to catch her dream. She knew that men had done this. She knew they were accomplished hunters. Wolves respect accomplished hunters, but she knew too, that she must avoid men. Men also made the forests of the wolf lands lie down and become tame. Wolves had not known before that the forests could be made tame, and they had not respected that aspect of men, therefore they had learned to distrust all men. Wolves do not like to live in a tamed place. They cannot understand why an accomplished hunter would want to make the forest tame, for taming a forest diminished the range and the numbers of that which can be hunted, diminished the colour, the beauty.

She would wait. She had the patience of glaciers.

She hunted when she was hungry, ate, returned, rested, waited.

She would not volunteer to die alone. That is not the way of such a wolf. So she must live until all her living strength was done, and such a wolf must also live with purpose. Her purpose was to make contact with other wolves. For the moment, for some days or some weeks, her life was waiting.

Time would change things.

Perhaps other wolves were making for Rannoch too, from the south and the west, a refuge for the pageant again.

If none came, she would travel again. She believed in travelling. But she also believed in the refuge of Rannoch and she would give it every chance to fulfil her purpose.

So there was no third dream yet. The two dreams told her that there were no wolves within reach. A third dream would tell her what she knew already. When wolves pursue a quarry that moves too fast for them they stop chasing. The dreaming, for the moment, had become a quarry she could not catch. She waited instead, and perhaps the too-fast prey would meet other travelling wolves and turn and come to her.

There had never been a time when the dreaming failed completely. She knew that wolves were fewer now, but there had been lean times before. No wilderness tribe is constant. They all ebb and flow, all rise and fall like winds, like rivers. There are low ebbs, black winds, droughts. Good springs and summers resurrect all their spirits. Wolves had recovered from hard times to hundreds before now. But more and more she found only the absence of wolves, and that absence was the only thing on Rannoch Moor that she feared.

Night without moon, cold as starlight, a thin black wind out of the north. She interrogated the wind, discarding its old and useless scents. She explored these:

Deer. Four hinds at a hundred yards. She heard the calf splash in the burn the hinds had cleared easily. She was not hungry, but she stared at the passage of the scent and her eyes discerned the darker black of their silhouettes.

Fox. On the move, east to west, farther off than the deer, and more pungent, and mingled with the entice-ment of a grouse, travelling in the same direction at the same distance and at the same speed, so dead in the jaws of the fox. The grouse excited her, and although she was not hungry she weighed the prospect of its suc-culence. But a fight with a fox was usually more trouble than it was worth, and if it was the dog fox heading for a tryst with the bitch, there would be two foxes to defend the grouse. If she had even one other wolf she could prise away the grouse, draw the two foxes, baf-fle and outrun them, and her accomplice would have made short work of the cubs. She discarded it all.

Eagle. Up there, beyond the burn where the deer crossed, but this side of the fox, a pair of golden eagles nested in an old pine tree. They were the beneficiar-ies of a hundred years of eagles, generations that had reinforced and added to the eyrie year on year so that even as the tree grew, the nest corrupted its shape as if a dark cloud had snagged in its topmost limbs. Winters usually burst apart the top of the eyrie and unpicked its foundations, but each year the damage was meticu-lously repaired and new walls added. Several times the whole thing had become top-heavy and its top half or its top two thirds had crashed to the woodland floor; and somewhere in its basement, the oldest timbers rot-ted through and the mass settled lower in the crown of the tree, redefining its own foundations. That April night the huge dark female (ebony and chestnut shades, golden nape) was sitting on two eggs; her mate, smaller (but only by golden eagle standards) and paler, roosted nearby on a taller tree. The wolf discerned their separate scents and the leftover bones of their prey. The male eagle, restlessly on watch even on such a night, and blessed with eyesight a wolf might envy, saw her clearly where she stood. Neither had any reason to trouble the other, but both had marked the passage of the fox, the grouse, and the likely presence of cubs.

Badger. In a shaded bank by a trickle of water that made slowly for the burn the deer had just crossed a small sett that sustained a handful of badgers. Nothing troubled the badgers, not even a wolf. There was nothing more unpredictable, nothing better equipped or better spirited to fight its way out of a corner than a badger. She had no reason to pick a fight with a badger, which had no reason to pick a fight with her. She gave the sett a wide, downwind berth. Whenever she met a badger, the two eyed each other warily, with mutual respect, and passed on. She also had an inherited memory of bears, although they had been absent from her landscape for several centuries. There was enough of the bear about the badger for the wolf to be cautious and avoid its company.

A new sound, a horse, slow on the hard track half a mile away; the rhythm of the gait told her it was being ridden. Horses on the track were usually being ridden. She knew the track now, travelled it in the dark for ease of movement, knew its horse scents and its people scents (the horse scent masked the people scent when the horse had a rider), understood its purpose. She also knew the groomed scent of a man's horse from a wild horse of

*the moor, their different sounds and rhythms and spirits;
and she knew and enjoyed the warmth between wolf
and horse, an ancient bond that was undiminished by
the horse's harnessing with people. She decided suddenly
to travel as far as the source of this slow horse sound.*

*She moved at an easy trot, her huge feet padding in
near silence among the pines, though the trees felt her
passage. The trees relished her presence in their midst
after a long absence as the tribe of wolves had thinned
out all across the land. The long-lived tree generations
were rooted in times of wolf plenty and tree plenty (for
the trees too were a dwindling race).*

*In that land of Rannoch, pinewoods and moor
together were the best hope for wolves, and therefore
for nature. Such compact logic was understood by all
creatures except men, for on the moor they had long
since become obsessed only with their own precarious
survival. They had misplaced the knowledge that their
salvation there lay in wild nature, and that the salvation
of wild nature lay in the wolf. Pinewoods and moor
together offered a place where wolves might withdraw,
heal, recover, begin again, a place from which they
might emerge fit to travel again. That recovery would
reawaken the old knowledge in all wolves, re-establish
Rannoch as a sacred place for wolves to which they
would return forever.*

*So the trees greeted the brush of her fur, the pad
of her feet, the warmth of her presence. Tree to tree,
they passed her through the darkness until she stood at
the edge of the clearing that accommodated the track.
The horse was travelling west and into the wind. The
wolf turned that way and followed, not using the track*

but travelling parallel to it, keeping a screen of trees between her and the clearing so that in her mind as she travelled she could see her own shape as one on the track might see it, and it was a shape made of broken shadows. For that she was grateful to the trees, and relished their presence in return, and in that spirit she closed on the horse and its rider, increasing her pace until she was level with the horse, and she fell in with the horse's pace, watching through the trees.

Suddenly the horse stopped and gave soft voice. The rider spoke: 'What is it?'

The horse stared at the trees. The wolf was a shadow among shadows. The rider stared too, but that shadowed confusion offered no explanation. Yet the rider thought something moved between the horse and the shadows, some warm air of communication that a rider might feel but not understand.

'Come on lass, I'm hungry. You're hungry, for that matter.'

The horse moved off at once then responded to the soft command for more speed.

The wolf had stopped when the horse stopped. She stood still now and listened to the diminishing sound, and knew that the horse possessed knowledge of her. The scent of the close-up horse and now the cooler scent of the rider lingered in her. She would know both again, the very horse, the very rider.

CHAPTER 12
Yellowstone

On so many days, we humans seem insatiable, determined to cobble together a fantasy in which there's nothing we can't have, can't own. But to a lot of wildlife watchers the wolf defies all that, standing as a link to the kinds of mysteries that lie well outside our pipe-dreams of manipulation and control. Seeing a wolf in the wild can feel like one of the final frontiers of nature – a frontier that can never be possessed.

– Douglas W. Smith and Gary Ferguson,
Decade of the Wolf – Returning the Wild to Yellowstone (2005)

THE NATIONAL PARK SERVICE did not end what was euphemistically known as 'predator control' until 1926. The great American wilderness was no such thing, because outwith Alaska, in what America calls the lower forty-eight states, the philosophy that 'the only good wolf is a dead wolf' was ubiquitous. The very phrase was a grimly pointed reworking of General Philip Sheridan's immortal utterance in the winter of 1868 to the Comanche chief Tosawi, who introduced himself to the General with the words 'Tosawi, good

160

Indian.' Dee Brown's *Bury My Heart at Wounded Knee* noted that the General's response was: 'The only good Indians I ever saw were dead.' Brown wrote:

> Lieutenant Charles Nordstrom who was present, remembered the words and passed them on, until in time they were honed into an American aphorism: The only good Indian is a dead Indian.

There is a curious parallel between Scotland and the United States of America in that subjugation of the human natives and the wolves seemed to go hand in hand, as if there were some unspoken recognition among their distant governments that the people might draw inexplicable sustenance from the presence of wolves in their midst. Many readers may well find that notion preposterous, but consider the quote from Smith and Ferguson at the beginning of this chapter: 'Seeing a wolf in the wild can feel like one of the final frontiers of nature – a frontier than can never be possessed.' Nothing was more intolerable to the London government of the eighteenth century or the Washington government of the nineteenth century than the idea of a frontier that can never be possessed.

Be that as it may, as the twentieth century struggled with its conscience through the pre- and post-war years, the pioneers of wolf conservation began to find a market for their ideas and their books. Aldo Leopold's now famous Road to Damascus moment in *A Sand County Almanac* was beginning to burn into the American folk-mind. He was young, he said, and 'full of trigger-itch'. 'A pile of wolves' that turned out to be cubs welcoming the return of an adult, appeared below the rimrock where he was sitting having lunch:

> In those days we had never heard of passing up a chance to kill a wolf. In a second we were pumping lead into the pack, but with more excitement than accuracy . . . when our rifles were empty, the old wolf was down, and a pup was dragging a leg into impassable slide-rocks. We reached the old wolf in time to watch a fierce green fire dying in her eyes. I realized then, and have known ever since, that there was something new to me in those eyes – something known only to her and to the mountain . . . I thought that because fewer wolves meant more deer, that no wolves would mean hunters' paradise. But after seeing the green fire die, I sensed that neither the wolf nor the mountain agreed with such a view.

Leopold's remarkable book, arguably the single greatest piece of nature writing ever, was published in 1949, the year after he died in a fire, and at a time when he was an adviser to the United Nations on conservation. How much healthier our wild landscapes might have been had he lived – and had the United Nations listened – is an idle speculation, but he had come to understand the place of the wolf in nature's hierarchy, and the necessity of its presence for the wilderness to be in good heart. The American architect Frank Lloyd Wright said that he did believe in God, but he spelled it Nature. If you hold with that illuminating idea, then you could do worse than have *A Sand County Almanac* for your bible.

Five years before its publication, Adolph Murie, the first serious wolf biologist, had published *The Wolves of Mount McKinley*, a ground-breaking work now regarded as a classic, not least because it was produced in a climate of wolf-hatred when pressure was being exerted by hunters to kill wolves inside the Mount McKinley National Park (now Denali) in Alaska. And some just went in and killed every pup in every den they could find anyway.

Nor was it just an American problem. This was how bad things had got:

> In 1968 . . . the grey wolf had just been listed as an endangered species in the lower forty-eight states; the Soviet Union had declared war on wolves; poisoning was still widespread across Canada; and the purity of the red wolf, which inhabits the south-eastern United States, was rapidly being eroded by an influx of coyote genes.
>
> Between public hatred and government extermination, wolves had disappeared from one-third to one-half of their former range, which originally included almost all the landmass of the Northern Hemisphere above twenty degrees latitude (which runs through Mexico City and Bombay, India). They were gone from much of western Europe and the more populated areas of Asia as well as from Mexico and the contiguous United States. If the wolf had any friends, it wasn't clear who they were.

So wrote another front-line wolf biologist, L. David Mech, in his foreword to a book called *Wolf Wars* by yet another, Hank Fischer. The book is the story of the plan to restore wolves to Yellowstone National Park, which straddles the northern US states of Wyoming, Montana and Idaho. It was a long and bloody campaign, arguably the most divisive in the troubled history of wildlife conservation anywhere in the world. Fischer's book was published in 1995, the year the first Canadian wolves were finally released in Yellowstone, but even at that defining moment the wolf wars were far from over. Fischer wrote:

> No one declared a truce in the wolf wars after wolves returned to Yellowstone Park and central Idaho. In fact, the battle cries grew shriller than ever. The Wyoming legislature, dominated by agricultural interests, welcomed wolves with a $500 bounty for anyone who managed to shoot one straying outside park boundaries. The governor vetoed the bounty but not the sentiment behind it. Montana's legislature responded with a resolution calling for the government to stock New York's Central Park with wolves. Idaho's new governor threatened to call out the National Guard to drive wolves from his state.

Conservation – principally in the shape of Defenders of Wildlife and the Sierra Club – had taken on the huge American agriculture industry and, suddenly, the White House; for in 1994, Congress went Republican after 40 years of Democrat domination, an era during which the Nixon administration had passed the Endangered Species Act and the wolf had been the first species to be listed. Fischer was the Northern Rockies field representative for Defenders of Wildlife from 1978 onwards. He developed the Wolf Compensation Fund and served on Congress's Wolf Management Committee. His persuasive testimony before Congress, in court, and at endless public hearings, became a powerful ally for the wolves' cause. He was a spectator among the huge crowds that gathered at the Roosevelt Arch to welcome the motorcade of government vehicles bringing the first wolves into Yellowstone.

It was a watershed. Conservationists all across the northern hemisphere celebrated and reasoned that if you could put wolves, of all things, back into the United States, anything was possible anywhere. Yellowstone shone its light into many murky corners of the world, and it still does. But in 1995, Fischer was not so sure. He had fought the wolf wars from the beginning and bore the scars. His book concludes on an almost weary note:

> Although historians may view Yellowstone Park wolf restoration as an important conservation milestone, it's not a particularly good model for endangered species recovery. The process took too long, was unnecessarily divisive, and cost too much. The United States has hundreds of imperilled wildlife species in need of help. Unless we adopt new tactics, our nation's efforts to conserve endangered species will fail.

His solution is to find a process that unifies rather than divides; political, industrial and conservation leaders who promote co-operation rather than confrontation, and whose organisations are hell-bent on finding answers. He quotes the biologist Paul Errington, perhaps the best-known 27 words out of the millions that comprise the copious literature of wolves: 'Of all the native biological constituents of a northern wilderness scene, I should say that the wolves present the greatest test of human wisdom and good intentions.' To which Fischer adds his last word: 'Bringing wolves back to Yellowstone Park certainly shows our nation's good intentions. But the test of our wisdom will be whether we allow them to flourish.'

Well, by the end of 2007, Yellowstone had 11 different wolf packs ranging in size from four wolves to 22, and a total of at least 171 compared to the peak figure of 174 in 2003. And 2007 was the first year since reintroduction that no new packs were formed, suggesting that the national park, with its superabundance of grazing animals including elk, moose, bison and deer, has all the wolves – or at least all the wolf territories – that it can handle. But in 2008, although the number of wolves had dropped to 124, there were 12 packs. One way or another, that sounds like flourishing to me.

A companion reintroduction in central Idaho, west of Yellowstone, a certain amount of dispersal that is inevitable given the wolf's propensity for travel, a slightly more relaxed attitude to the wolf thanks to Yellowstone's high profile and impressive public relations efforts on behalf of wolves, and the cross-border movement of Canadian wolves – all those factors have established a population of around 1,500 wolves in the three states of Idaho, Montana and Wyoming. A few have crossed into Oregon. That too sounds like flourishing.

Whether wisdom will continue to hold sway, time will tell. But what seems from this distance like a grotesque numbers game has begun, so that some critics of wolf reintroduction from the farming and hunting lobby say the numbers in the north-west Rockies states could be as low as 300 and still sustain a viable wolf population while the more optimistic scientists have argued for 2,000, and hunters have claimed that elk populations are declining due to wolves in a year in which they shot more than 22,000 elk in Wyoming alone. That kind of statistical feeding frenzy makes me squirm, but that may be simply because there is nothing in Europe to compare it with.

The decision of the Fish and Wildlife Service in 2008 to 'delist' wolves in the northern Rockies under the Endangered Species Act, and hand over wolf-management to the three states who found the original introduction scheme too politically hot to handle, made my eyebrows rise, but it was upheld in 2009 by US Secretary of the Interior Ken Salazar, with the conspicuous proviso that the wolf would remain listed in Wyoming because its law and management plans were not strong enough. But management of wolves will be turned over to state agencies in Montana and Idaho and parts of Washington, Oregon and Utah, plus the Great Lakes states of Michigan, Minnesota and Wisconsin.

My vote doesn't count in the United States of America, but I have always believed that you protect the strongholds with all the resources you can muster, on the simple principle that however a particular species fares furth of the strongholds there is always scope for subsequent expansion out from the strongholds if they are in good heart and good health. Delisting obviously reduces protection outside the national parks, and one newspaper report that came my way noted that between March and May 2008, the number of wolves killed by people in Wyoming, Montana and Idaho rose sharply to a total of around 70. One official at the Natural Resources Defense Council responded to the revelation thus: 'There's much greater public appreciation of the role of top carnivores. On the other hand, the myth of Little Red Riding Hood just won't die. It's amazing the pockets of fear and irrationality that still pervade the wolf debate.'

For all that, Yellowstone is a beacon. It is America's and the world's first national park, and celebrated as 'America's best idea'. (It was, of course, the idea of the emigrant Scot John Muir, which rather makes you wonder in a Leopold-at-the-UN kind of way the influences he might have brought to bear on the wild landscapes of Scotland had his father not decided to emigrate in 1849.) It is also a place of such sensation-rich beauty and tremendousness that whenever television casts its eye over it, as the BBC did in three memorable hour-long documentaries in the early spring of 2009, matter-of-factly giving the wolves their place amid tumultuous landscapes, the cause of wild wolves leaps effortlessly into the hearts and minds of millions on my side of the Atlantic Ocean. You watch, you are seduced, and the task of reintroducing wolves into your own country simply becomes an endeavour of the most self-evident wisdom. How could any clear-thinking person ever imagine that our mountains, forests, lochs, rivers and moors could ever be complete as long as the wolf is absent? And regardless of what new wolf wars may or may not lie ahead on the map of American domestic politics, Yellowstone has already done that, and people all across the northern hemisphere who crave a closer walk with wildness and wilderness are grateful.

It is one thing to watch the films. It is, of course, another to make the effort to meet wildness head-on. Doug Smith, leader of the Yellowstone Wolf Project, voiced his concerns in his remarkable account of the first ten years of wolf reintroduction, *Decade of the Wolf*:

> The vast majority of what people experience of nature these days, after all, comes from television. Entertaining, and even educational, as it may be, television flattens wildlife watching – purging the physical discomforts, removing all the time normally spent waiting for something to happen. Every inconvenience is left behind on the cutting room floor. The result is often a kind of tepid album of greatest hits, a non-stop string of events that even most of us working in the field see only a handful of times in our lives. While it's true that wolves show themselves frequently at Yellowstone, their appearance is nonetheless still in the context of the larger wild preserve – uncut, unedited. A person has to at least be willing to make direct contact with nature, to experience an unfolding of life that goes far beyond the animal he's come to see. In that sense wolf watching in Yellowstone is an experience of

nature much as it has always been ... As best-selling nineteenth-century author Henry George pointed out, the wild preserves of the West are critical, even for those who never set eyes on them. The mere thought of them, he suggested, tends to engender 'a consciousness of freedom'. To that end, the memory of wolves running like the wind through the Lamar Valley, or sliding down snowfields in fits of play, or even sleeping away a summer afternoon in the tall grass, can be a remarkable touchstone to that which makes our lives and our culture just a little more fascinating, a little more rich with wonder.

The Yellowstone wolves are the most watched in the world. Wolf-watching 'hotspots' have emerged along the road through the Lamar Valley, and the sheer number of visitors resulted in the Wolf Road Management Project with four objectives – human safety, wolf safety, visitor enjoyment and wolf monitoring and research. In the 117 days of the project from May–September in 2007, wolves were seen every day. The project team helped 32,600 people to see wolves, by far the highest number in the eight years of the project, but an independent research team from the University of Montana estimated the number of people actually seeing wolves was almost ten times that figure – 310,046. So watching wolves is not only public relations par excellence for the cause of wolves in general and wolf reintroduction in particular, it is also a major tourist attraction. The world beats a path to Yellowstone to see wolves, spends its money when it gets there, and spreads the gospel when it goes home again.

Northern hemisphere wilderness needs Yellowstone as never before, not just for its public relations value in the cause of the wolf, but also because it has created a unique opportunity to study the wolf. Because there were no wolves there for 70 years before 1995, the land had suffered the effects of that absence. Leopold had articulated the nature of the problem that the Yellowstone Project would inherit more 55 years later:

> I have lived to see state after state extirpate its wolves. I have watched the face of many a newly wolfless mountain, and seen the south-facing slopes wrinkle with a maze of new deer trails. I have seen every edible bush and seedling browsed, first to anaemic desuetude, and then to death. I have seen every edible tree defoliated to the height of a saddlehorn. Such a mountain looks as if someone had given God new pruning shears, and forbidden Him all other exercise. In the end the starved bones of the hoped-for deer herd, dead of its own too-much, bleach with the bones of the dead sage, or moulder under the high-lined junipers.
>
> I now suspect that just as a deer herd lives in mortal fear of its wolves, so does a mountain live in mortal fear of its deer. And perhaps with better cause, for while a buck pulled down by wolves can be replaced in two or three years, a range pulled down by too many deer may fail of replacement in as many decades.

After seven such decades, Yellowstone's mountain landscape knew all about that mortal fear. But one thing missing from Leopold's telling assessment of the problem was any experience of what would prove to be the solution – putting back the wolves. Almost from the moment the first wolves arrived, the staff of the Yellowstone Project became eye-witnesses to the unfolding effects of the wolf as a primary influence of biological change, change with an enormous reach down through the many-layered depths of the food chain to the very mountain grasses themselves. The very presence of wolves on the ground inevitably has a profound effect on prey species, but here was the chance to watch what happened as if it were a demonstration of the very forces that had shaped Yellowstone long before the white man came. The crucial change came in the behaviour of the huge elk herds. (Of 323 wolf kills detected by project staff in 2007, for example, 272 were elk.*) They began to abandon, or at least linger less long, in favourite grazing areas with no wide view. It had suddenly become important to see the surrounding land to avoid surprise attacks by wolves. What was happening was that the elk were remembering how to behave like elk again after so many sedentary years. As the northern part of Yellowstone gradually filled up with wolf pack territories, the elk were compelled to resume a life that is more or less constantly on the move. At a stroke, grazing pressures began to ease, and at a stroke, nature rushed in to fill the vacancy, unleashing all the diversity in its repertoire.

*The other species were eleven bison, seven wolves, four deer, three moose, two black bears, one pronghorn antelope, one golden eagle(!), one red fox, one otter and 'sixteen unknown prey'.

Willow was the first beneficiary, as willow so often is after ecological upheaval. Its recovery was swift – within the first three years – and decisive. That other great manipulator of the natural environment, the beaver, followed the willow. A beaver reintroduction scheme just outside the national park assisted a process that would have begun anyway, and beavers migrated into the park, lured by the abundance of willow. In the first decade of the Yellowstone Wolf Project, the solitary beaver colony in the north of the national park had become nine beaver colonies. What had begun was a process which, at its most spectacular, is called a trophic cascade, when a fundamental ecological change literally cascades right down the food chain from the top predators to the lowliest plants. Beavers build ponds, expand – or even create – wetland, a habitat that offers new homes for mammals as large as a moose and as small as a vole, for amphibians and reptiles, insects and wildfowl and songbirds, aquatic plants, grasses and flowers. These, added to the flowers that have begun to thicken again in regenerating grassland, are the first brushstrokes. The presence of wolves has begun to paint the mountains in new colours. The change is patchy at first, but once it begins, its progress is undeniable.

Other trees, notably cottonwood and aspen, have also begun to prosper again, more slowly than the willow, but once aspen regenerates in significant numbers, the most beautiful tree of the northern hemisphere brings all the shades of fire, the most audacious tints of the painter's palette, to the landscape.

Butterflies and moths and other insects arrive with the invigorated and diversifying vegetation, and songbirds not seen there in half a century contemplate the prospects of a new niche to fill. Science argues with itself about the point at which it can assert that a trophic cascade is finally and unarguably in place, but the process has begun, and unless America loses its nerve in the matter of wolves and scraps the Yellowstone Wolf Project that has won the admiration of the watching world, it can only go from strength to strength. This is the power of the wolf. This is how it paints mountains.

But the wolf has made one more impact on the ecology of Yellowstone, one that took the biologists by surprise. It is simply that wolves provide so much food for non-wolves. In *Decade of the Wolf*, Smith and Ferguson write:

> Thus far we've observed no less than twelve different species using prey killed by wolves . . . Biologist John Varley has dubbed this phenomenon 'food for the masses'. 'In all the planning, all the studies,' says Varley, 'the one thing we totally underestimated was how many other mouths the wolves would feed. Beetles and flies and mountain bluebirds – it's incredible.'

Beetles and flies and bluebirds, and ravens and magpies, black bears and grizzly bears (a grizzly can simply take over an elk carcase that wolves have killed, and often does), coyotes and foxes, golden eagles and bald eagles . . . and what's left after that lot have had their fill breaks down and seeps back into the soil as nutrients. There is no end to the benevolence of wolves. Yellowstone has taught us that too.

Scattered through the pages of *Decade of the Wolf* are portraits of individual wolves that have stood out in the eyes and minds and doubtless the hearts of those charged with operating the Yellowstone Wolf Project. There were number 14 and Old Blue, for example, in Chapter One, and then there was 293F in Chapter Three, and it is the life and death of that wolf that I return to now as I consider the potential of Yellowstone to influence the wider world. She was, you may remember, famous for leaving Yellowstone. She was a collared wolf, a two-year-old from the Swan Lake Pack near Mammoth in the north-west corner of Wyoming. One day in January, 2004, she walked off the radar and kept walking. It may have been that she left in search of a mate of her own and a territory of her own. It may have been that her lowly ranking in the pack offered her too few opportunities and she was one of those wolves that have what it takes to be a lone wolf for as long as it takes. Or it may be that she was one of those wolves that I think of as pilgrim wolves because they undertake extraordinary journeys, and at the end of their journey things are not quite the same as they were before. Perhaps she was just looking for a new mountain to paint.

By the spring of 2004, wolves had been reintroduced not only into Wyoming, Montana and Idaho but also into New Mexico and Arizona. It had begun to look as if Colorado was next. Historically, Colorado had been an important state for wolves. As the white man opened up the West in the mid-nineteenth century, estimates of almost 40,000 wolves were being bandied about, although there is no evidence that anyone ever tried to count them. Improbable as the number seems now, the size of the estimate suggests that the settlers were seeing a lot of wolves. A hundred years later there were none. But, by 2004, wolves were on the agenda in Colorado again, Rocky Mountain National Park was considering them as a solution to problematic numbers of elk and a Colorado Wolf Management Plan Working Group had been set up. It all seemed only a matter of time.

Then, on 7 June, a vehicle travelling on Interstate 70 near Idaho Springs struck and killed a wolf. It was 293F and she had travelled alone from northern Yellowstone, the better part of 500 miles. So, imagine you are one of the pro-wolf campaigners in Colorado, battle-weary from too many committee meetings, public hearings and the rest; you sit on the Wolf Management Plan Working Party, endlessly and slowly drafting and redrafting a plan for the distant day when the first reintroduced wolves finally shake off the encumbrances of the bureaucratic process (for all serious conservation endeavour is endless and slow; I often wonder what it is we are so afraid of). Then one day, a day beginning like any other, a wolf turns up dead on your doorstep having travelled 500 miles for the privilege. Coincidence or omen? Nature doing what nature does, or the divine intervention of some God-of-the-Wilds you didn't know you believed in until that moment? Perhaps you remember Frank Lloyd Wright's words: 'I do believe in God but I spell it Nature.' Is this what he meant?

Science, as represented by 293F's collar, allows you to retrace elements of her journey, and you assemble bits and pieces of it from what you know or what you guess of her route. She has survived largely on deer, which she has killed alone. Perhaps then, some long quiet evening hour, you marvel at the revealed nature of what it is you are trying to put back. Perhaps, after all, wolves will just walk back into Colorado uninvited in migratory pilgrimage, deftly avoid the trucks on I-70, and take the situation out of your hands.

Wolf 293F has assured herself a place among nature's immortals in the Rocky Mountains. She also became the reason for a book. *Comeback Wolves – Western Writers Welcome the Wolf Home* (2005) is an anthology in which, to quote its own publicity, '50 authors, ecologists, journalists, poets, activists and biologists gather their voices together in protest, praise, hope, and perseverance, all in order to raise awareness of the issues, past and present, surrounding wolves'. Such is the strength of America's enviably accomplished nature writing tradition.

I quote from Hal Clifford's essay in Chapter Three, but surely the most poignant page in the book is the dedication – *For Wolf 293F*. It is a wonderful excuse for such a book, and it is a very good book. And if there are 50 people in and around Colorado who can produce such thoughtful and diverse responses to the life (and one death) of wolves and have the whole thing published in one year, then I would urge every lone wolf in the American West looking for a place to settle to look no further than Colorado. Take care crossing I-70, but know you will be among friends.

Two of those friends will be George Sibley and SueEllen Campbell. Sibley teaches journalism at Western

State College of Colorado and Campbell teaches nature and environmental literature at Colorado State University (I await, as yet in vain, the day a Scottish university launches a degree course in nature and environmental literature!). Both are represented in *Comeback Wolves*, and their contributions made an impact on me for very different reasons.

Sibley's essay, slyly titled *Never Cry 293F*, is moving and funny and thought-provoking, not least in his unique take on the collars that science fits to many wolves. (Yellowstone, I was pleased to read, has guidelines for wolf-collaring, no more than 50 per cent of any one pack, and the wolf project declines to use ear tags. The reason is that many visitors like to see wild wolves looking wild. 'While we continue to place a high priority on gathering scientific information,' writes Doug Smith, 'so too do we need to be concerned about preserving the aesthetics of wild nature.') Sibley writes:

> My hope – a somewhat ridiculous hope, but those are the only serious hopes – is that somehow the wolves, consciously or unconsciously, will start adapting their capacity for intuitive communication to their radio frequencies, and will start broadcasting something that will help us know . . . something we need to know but so clearly don't. Yes, it is a long shot, but let's face it: our electronic extensions may be more sensitive than our natural ones these days, and we certainly spend more time and money transcribing and interpreting digital signals then anything else. If there were something coming through the wolf's collar, actually from the wolf, we

might find it electronically where we no longer can empathetically.

He wondered about 293F, and whether her collar might answer some of his questions.

It'd be useful to know what she thought when she left the Swan Lake pack, her family, her world. Was she asked or told to leave because the pack had outsized its territory? Do wolves actually have a sense of what they need to do to keep things in balance – even, or especially, to the extent of keeping themselves in balance? And even if they know that kind of thing, what were the feelings of the rest of the pack as they watched her leave, however necessary they knew it was? They are mammals like us; they don't just know things, they feel.

And why would I say we need that kind of knowledge from wolves? Because it is so clear that we are far, far out of touch with any balanced relationship with the universe, and maybe wolves are better at that than we are. Why else would we be inviting back fellow large predators that we'd earlier killed off, if not for some kind of consultation?

SueEllen Campbell's essay is a series of episodes covering several years. One, datelined Fairbanks, Alaska, stopped me in my tracks. She and a friend were teaching at a summer course on the University of Alaska campus:

We've read an essay about wolf trapping by local writer Sherry Simpson, and today she is visiting our class. Her essay is terrific – thoughtful, troubling, provocative, and complicated – but what really gets our attention is the wolfskin she's brought.

And why did that stop me in my tracks? Because I know that wolfskin. In fact, I know Sherry Simpson. I know that she keeps the wolfskin on the back of a rocking chair. I met her on the same university campus three years before SueEllen Campbell did while I was researching another BBC radio programme. Her essay was shown to me by another Alaskan writer, Nancy Lord, who advised my producer and me to make the time to interview her. We did. I wrote something of the result in a book called *Brother Nature* (2007.) She had told me she kept the wolfskin on the rocking chair and that she like to touch it and think about it. I asked her what it made her think. She said, 'It makes me think I could see more wolves in the wild. It's such an incredibly difficult thing to do. It makes me question my own values about things. I'm willing to eat things I didn't kill. I'm willing to wear fur I didn't trap myself, so it makes me wonder where I do stand on a lot of these issues. It's a great reminder of how there aren't really borders here but membranes, and you can cross back and forward between them all the time. That's what wilderness is here. I can live in a city and yet I can somehow cross through that membrane and be in wilderness just like that, and that's important to me.'

I made a symbol of her wolfskin. It became my shorthand for Alaska. Every time I fingered it in my mind I would startle at its hidden energy. I would question it and long to know more about it, long to feel on my face that keen northwesterly bearing scents and senses of that land where there are no borders, only membranes to pass through at will between the rocking chair and the wilderness.

The wolf enables all that, yet that is a by-product of its life, a casual but priceless consequence of the way it goes about its daily business, the business of just being a wolf. Tonight, sitting at my desk by the window that faces west into a Highland glen as early spring darkness begins to fall and the voice of the first snipe of spring sounds beyond the window, a turned page in a book written several thousand miles away has confronted me with the 12-year-old memory of a conversation I return to in my mind almost every time I think or write about wolves, and the name of the person with whom I spoke. And the book just happened to be a memorial to a wolf that travelled 500 miles alone and died, and in her dying, achieved the remarkable beginning of – what was your phrase, Mr Sibley? – some kind of consultation. If a wolf howl drifts in through this open window some spring evening as darkness falls and the first snipe calls, you will know the consultation has borne astounding fruit.

CHAPTER 13
A Dance with the Moon

SHE HAD FOLLOWED *the horse and its rider softly and at some distance as far as the edge of the wood. There she sat on a small rise studded with rocks and self-seeded pines a few inches high. She put her nose to the wind and stared out at the blue-black dusk that came in waves and lay in a miles-wide stillness all across the wild sprawl of the Moor. Its sky was blue-white and all but cloudless and first stars hung there.*

She questioned herself about horse and rider: about their unhurried presence so far out on the Moor, the easy bond between them, their complementary movements like the limbs of a single creature. Her eyes followed them until they faded into the dusk, blue-black themselves, as if the landscape had reclaimed something of its own, as if they belonged to each other and to that place, like wolves belonged to the pack and to the territory of the pack.

The shoulder of a mountain to the south was suddenly wreathed in gold, the first trappings of brightening moonlight. Her head swung towards it and stared. The moon heaved slowly clear of the mountain and stood above it, a fat oval. Its presence galvanised her. She flipped onto her back and writhed and squirmed like an otter in seaweed; she paused with legs raised and bent and splayed; she flipped onto her belly, tongue unfurled, ears cocked, eyes searching; she sprang to her feet; she snapped and chased at an imaginary quarry running in tight circles and figures of eight, leaning into every curve; she pounced on a piece of pine bark a foot long and snatched it in her jaws; she threw it ten feet in the air with a jerk of her head and ran and leaped to catch it; she threw it again and danced after it on two legs; she threw it again and let it fall to earth, watching as it fell and landed six feet away. The instant it hit the ground she leaped and crunched both front paws down on it, shattering the pine bark into a dozen scraps. Then she turned her back on it.

Black eyes watched her, the eyes of a mesmerised stoat. The more she cavorted the more the stoat was emboldened by curiosity. It advanced from the shelter of rocks in small ripples, then an abrupt two-foot stance, then more ripples. In a precise repetition of the leap that shattered the pine bark she broke the back of the stoat; then she ate it. Then she turned and walked back into the trees.

She stepped into a shallow river where the moonlight enlivened the ripples over a bank of shingle. Halfway across she stopped dead and stared sideheaded down at her front legs, ears cocked, entranced by the moonlight on the water and the patterns that broke and glittered round her legs then reformed and resumed their skittish jig with the moon. She turned her head from one side to the other. It was as if she were seeing something utterly new to her. It consumed her every sense and nerve-end, and for long moments only her head moved. Twice she lowered it to look *back between her legs at the water's advance; twice she looked directly at the moon, establishing in her mind the source of the sorcery. Then she began to race around in the shallows, snatching at the ripples with her jaws as if the lit crests of water were sinuous creatures she might catch. The game took over her life for perhaps ten minutes more, then she charged through deeper water like a bear chasing a salmon, then crashed ashore. She shook herself mightily, sending cascades of moon-bright droplets into the air, and in the process she invented another game. So she raced back into the water, charged ashore again, shook herself again, and this time she stopped abruptly to consider the effect of the moon on the airborne droplets. Three times more she repeated the madness, then she tired of it, and after a particularly hefty shake of her fur she raised her muzzle, tested the wind and vanished among the trees, a soundless darkening shadow among soundless darkening shadows.*

CHAPTER 14

The Absence of Wolves

There is something in my character that craves old simplicities, that goes looking for elemental things, that wonders how much my species has lost in its relationship with nature's other tribes, and how much of what is lost can be retrieved. When I go alone among mountains, among all wild places, I feel as if I am trying to repair an old and broken connection, like a bridge between landscapes. We broke it when we exterminated the wolf.

Again and again, walking the wolf-less mountains, I feel their absence, or rather I feel the distant and elusive nature of their presence, for no landscape that has sustained wolves ever loses completely the imprint of their reign.

– Jim Crumley, *Brother Nature* (2007)

BEN VORLICH, Perthshire, the summit on an afternoon of early July some old summer or other, and either the day before or the day after my birthday, I forget which. I also forget which birthday. I remember the ptarmigan and the deer, though. The day had settled warm and still after night-into-morning rain. Banks of thin and listless blue-grey cloud, tending to white at the edges, clung to the ridges and blurred the rims of the corries, softened and paled their hard shadows. The sun's ambition for that day was to banish all mountain cloud and grow hot, but two hours past midday the frail cloud still clung.

The only view in any direction was down. I was alone on the summit. I ate a late lunch, enjoying the solitude, the hill-quiet, the sun's hazy warmth. Highland Scotland does not throw up too many such days on its mountaintops in high summer. I had been still for the better part of an hour. I felt no urge to move. I could have gone down to the *bealach* between Ben Vorlich and Stuc a'Chroin and scrambled up the buttress to that other mountain summit standing upright in its own blue shadow over there above the paler blue void (I thought of Norman MacCaig's line 'gulfs of blue air'), but why bother? – the view wouldn't improve. The buttress in that light looked like something temporary designed to transform the mountain's appearance, the way a busby transforms the guardsman beneath. I had climbed it often enough to know its subtleties, to know where to push right whenever conditions were tricky, but it's not technically difficult climbing. Technically difficult climbing has never been among the reasons why I like mountains. No, the day would not be improved by climbing Stuc a'Chroin. But it might improve if I sat still. As Norman MacCaig put it (in the same verse of the same poem, 'High Up on Suilven'):

There are more reasons for hills
Than being steep and reaching only high.

There is a theory of mine at work here. It is that whenever I have reached a vantage point of any description in wild country without disturbing anything on the way, and if I have been more or less still and more or less silent for quite a while, then that time spent being still and silent is an investment that gathers interest as it lengthens, because I have succeeded in becoming a fragment of the landscape, and it is in that guise that nature is most inclined to come to me, to see what I'm up to. If you have the capacity for stillness that is willing to sacrifice most things for the reward of having nature come to you (I do – I take no credit it for it, but it is in me, perhaps a throwback inheritance from God knows what ancient member of the tribe), then sooner or later a mountaintop, for example, is likely to grow generous with its secrets.

Sit.

Be still.

Attune.

Let time pass.

Live for this moment alone in the very now where you find yourself, and if the mountain lays bare one of its secrets, be ready.

A noise over my left shoulder.

Damn.

I don't want noises. Mountaintop noises usually mean other people. I don't want other people, not here, not now. The noise again, a small scuffle, a throaty croak like a frog, but not a frog, not at 3,000 feet in July.

Of course! I know that croak.

I turned my head left, inch by inch, until the croaking one came into view, a cock ptarmigan, ten yards away, walking towards me. I neither saw nor heard the flight or the landing. How far did he walk to get here?

He advanced, turned left, walked towards the edge, stopped a foot away from where the mountain ended and the gulf of blue air began, and still ten yards away from me.

Then he sat.

Now I could watch him without straining over my shoulder. I saw him close his eyes briefly, a long, slow, sunlit blink. He had become what I hope for myself in this situation, a fragment of the landscape. He was a small rock. I usually aim to be a small boulder. I remembered Margiad Evans, an English nature writer, as I so often do in circumstances like these.

All good, true and loving earth writing must be done first out of doors, either spontaneously in the brain or roughly and livingly with the hand, then afterwards, as swiftly translated to permanent wording as may be. Translated to permanence – ah, is there, can there be permanence . . . The only chance is swiftness and intensity of feeling. Or else, as fallen snow obliterates all movement and knowledge, time lightens the impression and the precious secrets discovered are hidden moment by moment in the day of ever fresh discoveries . . . There is no substitute, even in divine inspiration, for the touch of the moment, the touch of the daylight on the dream.

I took the sentiment to heart years ago as a kind of gospel. It taught me, among other things, to pack a notebook and pencil and sharpener (pencil doesn't blot in the rain) in the top of my rucksack so that whenever I stop it comes out first and is ready. So I tried to write him down there and then while he sat and blinked his slow, sunlit blink, reminding myself of advice handed down by an American teacher of writing, Donald M. Murray – 'Never be embarrassed by crap first drafts.'

His red eyebrow is odd and overdone, and a startling shade at this distance, a piece of scarlet fuzzy felt left over from a nursery child's bird. The rest of him is mottle – interlocking fragments and shades of gold, brown, tawny, tan, grey, black on his widespread tail, white under his chin, patched on his flank like quartz, and on his folded wings . . . the wolf shades. Only a creature dedicated to stillness goes to so much trouble to transform its plumage four times a year. No creature is more *of* the mountain than a ptarmigan.

Ten minutes, punctuated by the slow, sunlit blinks. Is that how a ptarmigan sleeps?

He stirs himself, stretches out first one bright-white wing then the other, walks to the edge, steps off, boards the gulf of blue air, as fluent in the shapes of the mountain's airspace as in the shades of the stony ground; vanishes round a buttress.

Did he even know I was there?

I read it back: ' . . . *the wolf shades* . . . '

The ptarmigan's genius, like the wolf's, is to remain unseen until it declares itself, the ptarmigan to outwit its predators, the wolf to outwit its prey. Many, many times, in the north of the world, a wolf walks the high, stony places like this one where ptarmigan nest. The sitting bird can fly, of course, if she sees or hears the wolf coming, but that betrays the nest. She knows the wolf's way, because their tribes have evolved together for uncounted millennia. She knows the wolf knows she is there, or at least she knows she cannot rely on the wolf failing to notice her rock-stillness for what it is. But she knows too that the wolf often declines easy prey if that prey opts for stillness. It's as true for her as it is for the deer, the elk, the caribou, the moose, the buffalo . . . the big beasts all across the northern hemisphere that will sustain the whole wolf pack for days. The one with the courage to stand and face the wolf usually lives to tell the tale. It's almost as if stillness baffles the wolf, as if it's not in nature's script. The wolf likes its prey on the move.

So I wonder about that ptarmigan whose high-mountain terrain I shared for a few minutes, now that we are both natives of a wolf-less land; that ptarmigan that walked to within a few yards of me then sat and drowsed for ten minutes, my presence either unrecognised for what it was or undetected. And what I wonder is this: has the absence of the wolf these last 200-or-so years blunted the land-wariness of a creature like this whose principal predator now in a wolf-less landscape is the golden eagle? Out-of-control hillwalkers' dogs and the occasional forays of the hill fox up onto the high ground doubtless take a small toll (and neither of these have scruples about stillness), but the presence of the wolf is as a sharpening tool for the vigilance of all its prey species and all its fellow travellers. Does its long absence from its old territories, therefore, blunt that old vigilance? Do the prey species un-evolve to something less than their full potential?

Far down the mountain I saw white movement. In that light, even at a distance of over a mile, the tiny whiteness was a vivid intrusion on the natural order of the day. No ptarmigan would have sat beside such a shade. I put the binoculars on it, and it proved to be a white teeshirt with someone inside it, one of a small group of less conspicuous hillwalkers who had just turned uphill from Glen Ample into Coire Fuadaraich. Every eye on the mountain would see that shirt.

In all the time that I had been sitting high on the mountain I had not lifted the binoculars until that moment. I had not, for example, scoured the *bealach* or the corries on either side of it for signs of life – Coire Fuadaraich to the north-west, the Dubh Chorein to the south-east. I had been content with lunch, with the warm mountain stillness, with the random nature of my thoughts, with writing down the ptarmigan. Now, as I lowered the glasses and let my eyes wander over the lower slopes, the floor of the corrie began to move.

My first reaction was that such movement could only be achieved by a trick of the light infused by the heat haze, a kind of mirage. My second was to discount the first and focus the binoculars. All across the steeply-sloping floor of Coire Fuadaraich, hundreds of red deer were getting to their feet. There is no question in my mind that they had been disturbed by the white teeshirt. For as long as they had held their nerve, their heat-of-the-day stillness had served them well, so that even the herd's huge presence lay as undetected as a rock-still ptarmigan. But now they were restlessly on their feet, and unease went through the herd as an upstart breeze troubles the surface of a still pool. And for those few moments when that unease sought purpose and direction, their chaos of small movements was as eye-catching as a white teeshirt. Then the herd galvanised itself, all indecision done, purpose and direction determined. It chose flight and it chose to climb.

The corrie is tall and narrow. At its base was the source of unease and the deer sought distance from it, which meant not only the steep climb up to the *bealach*, but also a steadily narrowing climb. The highest deer turned to face uphill and began. The others, as widely scattered below them as the corrie allowed, crammed together behind them so that the whole mass of deer formed the shape of an inverted funnel that poured uphill. The lowest, furthest deer were almost stationary, but they had formed up like an army, waiting, while the first wave began to climb at the double.

The higher they climbed, the narrower and steeper the terrain, so the first wave grew slimmer and those compelled to fall back from its edges formed up immediately behind the leaders and the herd massing below made way for them, all of this forming and reforming at a steep uphill gallop. Then I heard them.

I sat directly above the *bealach*. That downward view now filled with a stampeding river of deer that flowed uphill. And as it flowed and the frontrunners strained up the last steep slopes below the *bealach*, it thundered. I had never heard such a sound before. It

rose on thermals of warm air like distant muted drumming, hundreds of drums. I guessed five hundred head
of deer, two thousand hooves, two thousand drums.
Their sound gathered and rose, a ragged concerto of
drumming that climbed the mountain by its airspace,
that seemed to arrive in my ears by way of my spine, so
that I felt myself straighten my back in response.

The herd changed colour as it climbed. Far down
in the corrie where the back markers had only just
begun to jostle uphill, the bright flood of haze painted
an orangey-yellow layer across their summer-red backs
and flanks, and in the growing heat, their hides shone.
But up at the head of the corrie where the walls of
the two mountains leaned closest and the air was bluer
and patched with broken shadow, the deer darkened to
woodier shades.

The front of the column reached the *bealach* and
crossed it no more than five abreast. I wondered if they
might pause there to reassess the threat of the white
teeshirt, but the momentum of the massed ranks at their
back was irresistible, and they charged across the level
ground headlong down into the Dubh Chorein without
breaking stride. And as they crossed and the hordes
followed, the thunder of hooves climbed not just the
airspace but throbbed up through the very rock of the
mountain, and because I sat on the mountain's uppermost rocks, through me too, and I shivered at its thrill.

As the front third raced downhill, the middle third
hit the *bealach*, and the final third charged up through
the narrows, the whole stretched out herd took on the
air of a single creature with a pliable spine, a colossal
snake, say, but a snake that thundered as it slithered.

Then the last of them was over the *bealach* and not one paused to look back, and the sound dwindled away and the sun lit the backs of the last few, and the sound of them was replaced by the scent of them, for that too had climbed the airspace on the thermals and lay as a cloud about the summit rocks. Then silence rushed in and two hillwalkers appeared by the summit cairn. One waved and pointed, and called out, 'Did you see the deer?'

I waved back and smiled and nodded, but the thing was done and no words came. The walkers headed off for the further cairn along the mountain's short summit ridge. I picked up my notebook and pencil and wrote down the first words that came into my head, even though they were not my words:

> There are more reasons for hills
> Than being steep and reaching only high.

High up on Suilven or high up on Ben Vorlich, it is surely one of the great truths of all good, true and loving earth writing.

The white teeshirt and its muted companions did not climb the mountain. Their expedition seemed to stall when they mobilised the deer. When I finally left the high ground I saw them retreating far down the glen, the unwitting originators of what I still consider to be one of the more extraordinary hours of my life. Whatever they may have seen and heard from below, it was surely beyond their comprehension to envisage how the flight of the deer herd looked and sounded and smelled from above.

I will remember it forever.

A little while after the event, I made an interesting discovery about the corrie. Fuadaraich – it is a very unusual name. Many corries have simple names that recur all across the landscape – Gaelic words meaning rough, for example, or rocky, or a particular colour, or a species of tree, or a place where deer calve, that kind of thing, practical names that describe the landscape perfectly. But I never came across another Coire Fuadaraich. One day I went in search of its meaning. I am no Gaelic scholar, and I have that little learning of the language that is a dangerous thing. But it has named most of my preferred landscapes and so it intrigues me. And although I have found no reference to the precise spelling of *fuadaraich*, Gaelic spelling on OS maps made in Southampton was ever an inexact science. In fact the spelling of all written Gaelic of a certain age is alarmingly flexible. *Fuadaraich* is close enough to *fuaraich* to be worth considering, and *fuaraich* is a verb meaning to cool or to become cool, and *fuarachadh* (the same sound with the addition of an inconsequential final 'uh' syllable) is a noun meaning the act of cooling, relief from heat. And I thought then how in the heat of that early afternoon all the deer were lying down in a corrie named for the act of cooling, of relief from heat, and it could not fit the circumstances more perfectly.

The deer knew the corrie as a place to lie up in oppressive warm weather, and so would the shieling folk of Glen Ample who doubtless named that landscape. And so would its wolves. One effect of the presence of wolves on the ground is to manage deer herds with the kind of relentless efficiency that we (as the only species that now manages deer) could never begin to emulate. A wolf pack is more or less constantly on the move within its territory, and for that simple reason, deer are more or less constantly on the move too. The absence of wolves these last two centuries has made the deer more or less sedentary.

The absence of native trees in Glen Ample is a direct consequence of the absence of wolves, and the browsing of hordes of sedentary deer. In the days of the wolf and the fewer, more mobile deer, the glen was lightly wooded – birch, rowan, a few pines and aspen; alders on the burn are all that have survived. A fairly brutal intrusion of dense plantation spruce high on the west flank of the glen around 30 years ago was not what nature had in mind. The map still marks 'Coille Baile a' Mhaoir' a mile to the north of the lower slopes of Coire Fhuadaraich, and *coille* is the Gaelic word for a wood. No tree dignifies the place now.

Suppose, then, the half-a-dozen walkers with the white teeshirt in their midst had been a pack of as many wolves, and perhaps three hundred years ago. The wolves would have had light woodland on their side, and in that circumstance they were all but invisible when they chose to be. The accidental effect achieved by the appearance of the walkers would be precisely the effect desired by the wolves. But they would have come in a fan from below the deer, and the deer would have run as they ran from the walkers. But whereas the walkers provoked an orderly retreat, with the herd bunching behind the leaders and the back-markers slowed to a trot perhaps twenty or thirty abreast, while the front of the herd galloped five abreast across the *bealach,* the wolves panicked the back-markers and scattered them wildly, and with the deer both trying to run and hemmed in by the corrie walls, the wolves made the easiest of killings. And whereas the walkers scared the deer out of the corrie of cooling for a few hours (after which they would wander back and resume the browsing-to-the-bone of the treeless glen) the wolves' instinct for travel had the crucial effect of keeping the deer herd constantly on the move.

This teaches you two things about red deer. One is that in the days of wolves, the deer were travellers too because the wolves insisted on it, so there was far less scope for the lame and the old and the sick to survive; the herd was smaller and healthier because the wolves insisted on that too. The other is that the red deer is at least every bit as much a woodland animal as an animal of the bare hillsides. John Buchan wrote in his famous 1924 novel of the Highland deer forest, *John Macnab*:

> Great birch woods from both sides of the valley descended to the stream, thereby making the excellence of the Home beat, for the woodland stag is a heavier beast than his brother of the high tops.

In those parts of mainland Europe where red deer still live mainly in forests you find stags a third bigger than the Monarch of the Glen and his kin. So by keeping deer on the move the herd is smaller, the animals larger and healthier, and woodland flourishes to such an extent that it becomes forest and a healthy forest can sustain a healthy deer population. The agent that makes all this possible is the wolf. It bears repeating: in a northern hemisphere wilderness, with the wolf in place everything in nature makes sense, but in the absence of wolves nothing in nature makes sense. We have taken upon ourselves the role of the top predator, and such is our inefficiency in the job that we first eliminated nature's genius of biodiversity in the wolf, then instructed the landscape to evolve as a bare land overrun by deer and sheep, then – a last madness – we invented a forestry industry to grow trees nature would not have chosen and in a way that nature would never have chosen to grow them. And then we shut the deer out from these forests.

So there was an old early July afternoon and early evening the day before or the day after my birthday and I was walking back south down Glen Ample, my head full of the deer and the sight and the sound and the smell of them, and as I walked out to where I had left my car I was redesigning the glen in my mind so that it looked not as it once did but rather as it could look with only a little realignment of landowning policy, a little willingness to accept the failures of past and present regimes, and the colossal miracle that will be required before your species and mine acknowledges one essential truth: that the wolf will do the job better than you or me.

There are three small summits on the glen's blunt western ridge, all named by the Gaelic language, all saying exactly what they mean. The northmost is Meall nan Oighreag, which is the hill of the cloudberry, and sure enough, cloudberry grows vigorously there. The middle one is Sgiath a'Chaise; *sgiath* is a wing and *caise* is steepness and sure enough the summit is wing-shaped and the steepest contours on that side of the glen cram around it. The third is Meall Mor, which more or less means the big lump, and, especially seen from down on Loch Lubnaig, it is exactly that. Between the Wing and the Lump there is a crag whose name is Creag a' Mhadaidh, which is the Wolf's Crag, and while, as we have already seen, names on maps that insinuate the once-upon-a-times of wolves are as biologically reliable as Aesop, there is a stronger case to be made where the surrounding landscape has been named with such precision. There is, for example, many a Creag na h-Iolaire – the eagle crag – hereabouts where eagles still perch or nest as they must have done for centuries, many a Creag an Fhithich – Raven Crag – that still resounds to the loud proclamations of ravens. And there can be few places in the whole of Britain further removed from the influence of Viking or Saxon than Highland Perthshire, so none further removed from their Wolfs and Ulfs and Olafs that doom so many folklorists to disappointment when they go looking for genuine wolf place names. Nor is there a local last wolf tradition, no historical perversions of hunter-heroism that invite ridicule like Strath Glass, Sutherland, and the Findhorn. And when you watch the deer on the run within their own landscape, watch how they use it and watch how they are constrained and made vulnerable by it, there is, at the very least, a sense of the wolf at work in such a landscape, and the presence of a Creag a' Mhadaidh perhaps acquires a degree of credibility.

The glen subsided into a sultry early evening, a seductive mood of edgy, unrelaxed tranquillity, as though perhaps there was a storm under the horizon but heading this way. I had seen something in a flock of whooper swans a few months earlier that had sown that particular seed. I had stopped to watch them from my car where they grazed in a field, the car partially screened by a skinny hedge. The birds were relaxed and grazing, untroubled by my presence. I had been there for about half an hour when suddenly every bird stood erect, heads held high, facing west. I swivelled the binoculars to see what might have alarmed them; anything from a dog-walking farmer to a passing white-tailed eagle might have induced such a spontaneous and unanimous response. I found nothing. Still the disquiet flowed through the flock like a wind among fallen leaves. They called constantly for fully ten minutes before a crack of thunder and a shaft of lightning heralded a short and ferocious storm that blackened the visible world, whitened the ground with hailstones and rocked the car with gusts. No hint of the storm had offered itself to me, but the swans had known about it while it was still under the horizon.

In my Perthshire glen on a summer's evening a few hundred feet below the Wolf Crag, then, I felt some unnameable disquiet, and I thought of the swans and the storm. And I had just been handed a vivid enactment of the effect of the absence of wolves, and in the midst of it all there was a crag named for a wolf. I can't see storms under the horizon; yet I was picking up on something apparently still out of reach. It would take much longer than it took the swans to sniff out the storm, but in time I realised that my nature writer's sensibilities were responding for the first time to the crackling energy of the sense of a wolf *presence* in my own landscape. And that was what had been the root of my disquiet.

I walked out and drove home. There was no storm that night, and the morning after dawned clear as the headwaters of the Allt a' Choire Fhuadaraich, the burn of the corrie of cooling, where the deer sought sanctuary and relief when a midsummer midday grew uncomfortably sultry, and wolfishly edgy.

For nineteen consecutive Tuesdays of summer and early autumn a few years ago, I gave a series of talks to groups of American visitors on a ship purpose-built to cruise between Inverness and Oban by way of the lochs and canals of the Great Glen. Each Tuesday she berthed for the evening at the top of the tumultuous series of canal locks near Fort William known as Neptune's Staircase. I drove from Glen Dochart, where I was living at the time, by way of the Blackmount, the edge of Rannoch Moor and Glencoe, boarded the ship, had a meal with the people who would be my audience, did my talk about the landscape and wildlife of Highland Scotland, then drove home.

It was an agreeable and well-paid assignment, and that late-night drive home became a delightful ritual, the job done, the adrenalin of performance cooled, the landscape as remarkable as anything you can drive through the length and breadth of the land, the roads empty. I would drive through Glencoe somewhere around midnight, and often my car was the only wakeful movement in a still and slumberous world. I became familiar with the wheel of the stars across that portion of Highland sky, the coming and going of the moon, and on the long straights south-east and south after the night-black pyramid of Buachaille Etive Mor, the unfailing presence all along the roadside of hundreds of red deer. They walked, stood, and often lay all over the road, and moved off reluctantly at the approach of my car. They came down to the road at that hour to graze the lush grass of the verges and to moonbathe on the warm tarmac of the A82. (I thought of the wolf on I-70.) Their eyes stared back weirdly at the passing headlights, but I was always aware of the shadowy shapes of the hordes just beyond the range of the lights. So I developed the habit of stopping in a lay-by, switching off everything, opening the windows and letting the silence and the darkness rush in.

Eyes and ears take time to readjust to the demands of such drastically changed circumstances. I found eventually that it helped to sit for a couple of minutes with my eyes closed, then when I opened them the night was a bright place. By then, too, my ears had begun to accommodate the unsilent night, the conversations of a relaxed deer herd, the yap of a fox, the moans of owls, the quiet passage of water, the layers of pitch that make up the voice of an easy breeze.

Soon the car became a part of the landscape, albeit one that didn't smell like it, and the deer treated it accordingly. That is, they ignored it, they walked round it, often no more than a couple of yards away, but never closer than that. They grazed nearby, they muttered to each other. I guessed that even with the windows open the smell of the car masked the scent of the animal within, and as long as I stayed quiet and still and inside, they were quite untroubled.

I had no wish to trouble them, it was enough to sit still among them for a few minutes, using only my night eyes to try and make them out, to distinguish size and characteristics of individuals. Besides, I was dressed for after-dinner conversation on a cruise ship, not for the fine line the A82 treads there between the mountains of the Black Mount and the colossal night-blackness of Rannoch Moor, where, in my own mind, Scotland's last wolves surely worked the deer herds and for many years outwitted the outrageous determination of mankind to wipe them from the face of the land, once and for all.

Sitting there alone with the night and surrounded by the complacent deer, I harboured the thought that yes, mankind wiped the wolf from the face of the land once, but not once and for all; that here is surely where the wolf's story should begin again.

Once, I wondered what effect it would have on the deer if I bought a CD of wolves howling, and if I slipped it into the car's CD player and cranked up the volume and let that ancient anthem of the landscape loose again through the open windows. What dim inheritance might stir in the breast of a red deer then? But I baulked at the artificial basis of the notion, and I have never gone back to sit among the deer an hour after midnight, never bought the CD. I'll wait for the real thing to come along, as sooner or later it surely will.

But I know that it was out there, in the careful embrace of Rannoch Moor, that a single wolf lingered, alone until age and loneliness finally defeated her, and she spent her final days trying to make contact with

others of her kin by the only means left to her when
travel and howling had failed. Then I thought that they
may say the last Caledonian wolf is dead, but the truth
is she is not yet born.

CHAPTER 15
A Dark Memory

TREE BY TREE she travelled the morning, deeper into the Black Wood of Rannoch, higher too, for the Black Wood reached many miles to the south and west, feathered the slopes of many hills and mountainsides with pale and dark blue-green and bottle-green plumes. She skirted a wide, boggy clearing with scattered heathery hummocks. The pines in the bog were poor and skinny; they fared ill and died young. On the knolls they prospered in ones and twos, heftily limbed and wide-crowned. But her gaze was held by a solitary rowan. Its short, thick trunk tilted away from a cluster of rocks about its roots. Its branchy spread was even and rounded. A thick, vivid green fur of moss that covered the rocks had spread to the lower trunk, ending in a dead-straight diagonal across the trunk, the same angle at which the tree leaned. The tree had grown straight, then leaned in later life in response to some upheaval among the rocks, or the encroachment of the bog.

The rocks formed a corner from which the crumbled base of old walls emerged low and straight and at right angles. The bright grey of the rock showed here and there through many decades of gathering moss and lichen: a house, another refuge of the Broken Men, the rowan deliberately planted to fend off malevolent forces, a forlorn hope on the edge of Rannoch Moor.

Then she tired of the rowan and a new mood took hold of her. She pranced on her hind legs a few paces, touched down lightly on her front paws and sprang into the air to land again on her hind legs, a giddy dancing moment of play. She pawed at a butterfly, the first of that spring, then leapt to snap her jaws at it, but it swithered out of her reach. She stopped abruptly and looked round to see if any watching eyes had noticed her antics, found none.

She turned uphill then and walked on, skirting the clearing, keeping to the lightly spaced trees around its edge. The trees, the fitful sunlight, their shadows, all broke up the travelling shape of her into meaningless fragments, a shape that moved at the edge of things, a shadow among shadows, soundless as butterflies, defeating even eagle eyes.

She started to move west. She crossed the high ground of Cnoc Eoghainn and the glen beyond, skirted the conical hill of Leagag by the oakwoods of its northern slopes. Oakwood light is quite different from pinewood light, especially in that tight-budded northern spring. The pines clothe the slopes in crowds of overlapping crowns like the feathers on furled eagle wings. But oaks insist on their own space, clothe the slopes in far-flung branches like herds of stags. In winter and spring especially, sunlight lies on the floor of the oakwoods in dark-edged pools. She moved through these pools and their shadowed edges and her grey and black and pale tan fur shone and then faded, shone and then faded, and she walked on, and then she left the

oaks behind and was back in the lightest of the pinewood again as the trees thinned, and then she began to
catch the scents and the sense of the open moor itself.

She remembered the horse suddenly. She remembered its pale, grey-gold sturdiness, the sense of its
ancient wildness that still beat as a second heart, for
all that it did its rider's bidding. It had also been alert
to her presence. She splashed into the tumbling waters
of Gleann Duibhe, the Black Glen, the last westward
gesture of the Black Wood before it succumbed to the
big winds that scoured the moor. She lay down in a
shallow pool and lapped water and sunlight.

And then there was a darker memory. The shouts
and stench of men, the high-pitched wail of the big
hounds that stood taller than her by a head and ran
like gusts of fast winds; the horses, a row of advancing
hooves blocking the natural line of escape. The wolves
had scattered and turned, taking their chances with the
hounds and the blades and clubs of the men. But she
alone had run on straight at the horses, ran straight for
the hooves of the biggest horse, and even as its rider
leaned at her with sword arm raised, the horse shied
away from her, giving her space, and she went through
that space as a falcon moves through air. For horses
work not just in partnership with people, but also with
that loyalty to wildness that sustains wolves. Faced
with the running wolf, the horse adhered to that older,
original loyalty.

So she had run through the horses and on into the
deepest, darkest recesses of that Strathspey pine forest
with no backward glance at the blood-letting of the
hunt. The pack's best chance was to scatter widely and

divide the hunt into fragments. But the hunt had chosen its time and place and strategy carefully, and turned out in force. The first encircling rush killed three, and maimed two others. One more was pursued by three hounds, caught by the throat on the hillside and torn apart, but it killed one of the hounds in the process. Then the hunt reassembled and went scouring the country for the possibility of survivors.

She had heard the hounds again, loud and closing. She came to a river. She jumped into a deep pool darkened by overhanging branches, and swam to a shallow ledge at its upstream edge. She slithered onto that rocky bed and let the weight of the water press her into it, submerged her head and lay there with only the tilted tip of her muzzle above the water, breathing. She wanted to gulp air, to pant, but stone stillness and ruthless, painful control of her breathing was her only chance to live. The water, the branches and the fluctuating light, broke up her shape, the water killed her scent. So neither sight-hound nor scent-hound discerned her.

To be a shadow among shadows, to move at the edge of things, these were the things that gave her life meaning, and she was unusually accomplished at both. She alone survived the hunt. And alone was how she travelled from Strathspey to Rannoch. And the memory of it all had resurfaced when she lay down full length in a shallow river pool by the edge of Rannoch Moor.

She shook off the memory of the hunt as she shook off the waters of the Abhainn Duibhe. She walked west until she had left the living trees behind, although there, out on the high, bright edge of the Moor of Rannoch, she walked among the bleached bones of the corpses of trees that once shaded even the gaunt bareness of the Moor. She sat there for a sunset hour above herds of ambling deer, watched the reddening sun blaze low over the heave and sprawl of the Moor, burnished by loch and lochan, grizzled by smashed rock in every imaginable form, defended by the blades and barbs of its own wildness. She moved again in the dusk, still west, away from the memory of trees into a land as treeless as oceans. In another hour she walked side by side with her own moonshadow, with nature at its most demanding and its most accommodating, for what was she but a mobile fragment of the one true wilderness where she walked?

CHAPTER 16
Rannoch Once More

I have sat long and often and listened to the ancient river speech, to the windsong of three birches and a rowan, the rowan above a meeting of waterfalls, which should be a portentous place. And the word on the wind and in the speech of the river is that the trees and the wolves and the people will be back.

– Jim Crumley, *Something Out There* (2002)

I HAVE RETURNED to the high bright edge of Rannoch Moor. I have had it in my mind for a long time now that this is where to restore wolves to Scotland.

Why here?

In the first place it is wild, if not exactly wilderness. With the addition of wolves it could reincarnate as wilderness. They can do that. Rannoch Moor is more or less empty of people, and for a while at least, it will be important that the wolves are not disturbed by people while they find their feet in the new territory, although I imagine they will recognise it at once as an old wolf territory. Nor, I suppose, should people be disturbed by the wolves for a while, although that will change, and soon enough the people will come hundreds of miles for the remote prospect of seeing and hearing wolves.

I have heard it said again and again that you cannot reintroduce wolves without a widespread education programme, and maybe there is a certain amount that can be done to prepare the ground, but in truth the only way to be educated about wolves is to allow them into our midst, to give them space and time, and to watch and learn from them. They owe us nothing, we owe them everything. What we did to wolves would be called ethnic cleansing if we had done it to people.

In the second place, Rannoch Moor is high and wide-open, which means it has long, hard winters. Wolves are designed for long, hard winters and prosper while their prey species weaken. It simply never gets too cold for a wolf.

In the third place it has food, specifically red deer. Studies in Europe and America have shown that if you reintroduce wolves from an area where their main prey species is deer or elk or moose or buffalo, they bring that preference with them and it transfers down through subsequent generations. So we reintroduce European wolves accustomed to red deer, and having conspicuously failed in recent years to reduce red deer populations to numbers that the land can sustain, we can watch how wolves do it.

In the fourth place, it is central. Out-on-a-limb wolf populations (especially reintroduced wolves) isolated on an island or in a coastal corner of the landscape are vulnerable to disease and attacks from people; there will be some people who will resist the reintroduction – with wolves there always will be.

In the fifth place, I have an instinctive idea, quite unsubstantiated by any shred of evidence, that the last of our wolves died old and alone on Rannoch Moor. I have learned to trust such instincts, the ones that have been honed by the long years of wandering the land and sitting still with the land and watching. In an earlier book, *Brother Nature*, I wrote about interviewing the late Don MacCaskill, one time head forester of Strathyre Forest in Perthshire, an exceptional wildlife photographer and an enlightened naturalist. The occasion was a radio programme about reintroducing lost mammals and the subject of the interview was the beaver:

So we stood on the wetland shore of Lochan Buidhe, a reedy little watersheet to the north of Loch Lubnaig frequented by otters and herons and wintering whooper swans, and an occasional resort of the mute swans from the loch. There were four of us that spring morning, Don and I, BBC producer Dave Batchelor, and a man who had worked with beavers in France, and I interviewed my old friend. It was he who had brought us to the shore of Lochan Buidhe.

Here, he said, was where we should introduce beavers.

Why here? I asked. I expected a naturalist's assessment of habitat, food supply, lack of disturbance, that kind of thing. And perhaps a photographer's assessment too, for he lived nearby and would have loved to be involved in such a project. But instead he said: 'I had a dream they were here.'

At which point the man from France smiled and nodded vigorously and said: 'I am impressed. Do you know, this is so like the landscape in France where we reintroduced beavers.' He nodded again. 'So like it.'

I go often to Lochan Buidhe, and almost as often I think about Don's simple conviction that his dream validated the idea of beavers here. And the more I think about it the more it impresses me too. Because there would have been a time – even among these very hills – when the assistance of dream or second sight or some knowledge acquired intuitively from some realm beyond reason would have informed decisions and determined the course of events. Seers and sages, sung and unsung, are part of the history of such places.

North American Indian and Inuit cultures are rich in such traditions, and we often know more about them because they stayed closer to nature for much longer than we did (and in some places they still do), and because America's admirable tradition of nature writing has written them down and found a market place in modern popular culture. Don lived his life in nature's company . . . and if you spend your life working with nature on nature's terms, determined to live as close to it as is humanly possible today, it is far from fanciful to suppose that nature in return might trust you and use you to further its cause, and insinuate its purpose into a dream.

And if you take that philosophy and present it to such a body as, say, Scottish Natural Heritage, or the petitions committee of the Scottish Parliament, and suggest that it is a more appropriate basis for action on behalf of wildlife than their ponderous bureaucracies, how far do you think you would get?

And yet consider this. The dream was simple and specific – a particular species in a particular landscape. The pedigree of the dreamer was impeccable. His knowledge of nature was gathered in nature's company, much of it in the landscape of the dream. On the basis of that knowledge, he was permitted to design forestry plantations and change the ecology of mountainsides. He was accustomed to thinking deeply about reintroducing species, especially those that inhabited a treed environment. I had heard him discuss the notion many times. If that substantial store of intimate knowledge and careful reason was then infiltrated by a simple and vivid dream, why would you not be justified in trusting it utterly as a thing of profound significance and defining purpose?

I dare them.

I dare the ponderous ones at SNH and the occasionally surprising ones at the Scottish Parliament to act on Don MacCaskill's dream. Let them have their scientific trial by all means, radio-collar and ear-tag their beavers if they must, and follow their every waking, sleeping moment and cull them if they get out of hand or if the project takes cold feet, make their scientific appraisals and chunky reports and collect their salaries. But allow the dream too. Allow beavers to be wild here at Lochan Buidhe, untagged, uncollared, and allow nature to make the decisions, and leave those of us who still believe in the natural order to watch and wonder at what unfolds, at the revealed purpose of nature in choosing a man like Don MacCaskill to be the seedbed of a dream.

The example of people like Don is relevant to the reintroduction of wolves. If he had been a tribesman in the Oglala Sioux, his belief endorsed by Black Elk, he would have been a tribal legend. But he was born in Kilmartin, Argyll, and he worked for the Forestry Commission where his concerns for the natural environment at the expense of commercial expediency frequently fell foul of the system. He had faith in his instincts and these were invariably informed by knowledge gleaned at nature's beck and call. He raged against a proposal to plant the upper reaches of a nearby glen where golden eagles nest, arguing that it would wreck a crucial part of the eagles' hunting territory. He was overruled by headquarters, and eventually designed the planting programme himself. A few years after his death, when it became clear that he had been right, the trees were removed.

So when I go to Rannoch Moor with wolves on my mind and feel the rightness of the place and the power of the instincts that have led me there, I remember the example of Don and I trust it. I did not dream it, exactly, but the conviction grew in me over time, and in the American tradition of nature writing I admire so much, I wrote it down. It seems to me now that the time is right for Scotland to make a leap of faith on nature's behalf. We have created two national parks – the Cairngorms and Loch Lomond and the Trossachs – and by any rational assessment of the service they have rendered to nature they have failed utterly. So now we know what not to do. But the parks exist, they have been set aside as different, they are allocated state resources, and if only the philosophy of these two parks can be swayed towards protection of native habitats and wildlife, and if the parks can be joined by a third park with Rannoch Moor at its centre and dedicated to re-establishing something like wilderness, then the opportunity exists to let the influence of the wilderness core seep south-west into the northmost part of Loch Lomond and the Trossachs National Park, and north-east into the southern reaches of the Cairngorms National Park. This third Heartland National Park will stretch from Glen Dochart and Loch Tay in the south to the Monadhliath in the north, which by Scottish standards is vast, and it will cement in place a wedge of Highland landscape, a threefold national park dedicated to the wellbeing of nature. The core of this is the place to reintroduce wolves so that once they establish themselves they can spread out into other landscapes set aside for the principal purpose of nature conservation, and as we have already seen, they will transform the landscape as they go. So that is why Rannoch Moor, that is why I returned here to watch it on a cold bright day of early spring, 2009, and to dream my wolf dream.

As I drove north towards Rannoch, I caught myself rehearsing old arguments, cross-examining myself, and ultimately wondering if Scotland will ever have the courage to put wolves back, wild wolves, into a landscape set aside specifically for the purpose, and strictly on the wolves' terms, rather than on ours. The European Union Species and Habitats Directive of 1992 obliged the British government to consider the possibilities of reintroducing extinct species, including the wolf. The Scottish government assumed that responsibility in 1999, but has done little towards fulfilling that obligation. It is also safe to assume that situation will not change unless European law acquires bigger teeth, a bit more bite.

Or perhaps something unforeseen will happen to galvanise public opinion. Meanwhile there are straws in the wind. There is a pro-wolf organisation, the Wolf Trust, that campaigns for their reintroduction. More mainstream conservation organisations discuss the notion more readily than even ten years ago, and watch the slow shift of wolf populations in western Europe with interest. And Yellowstone has become a catalyst for wolf-related endeavour everywhere, even here. When Yellowstone biologist John Varley remarked that they had had no idea that the wolf could feed so many other mouths, providing 'food for the masses', he may not have realised that the example of Yellowstone in turn feeds the hunger of so many frustrated wolf enthusiasts all across the northern hemisphere

There are wolves in Scotland today, of course, in zoos and wildlife parks, notably at the Highland Wildlife Park at Kincraig in Strathspey and a kind of Highland campus for Edinburgh Zoo. By definition, they are wolves inside a fence, and a wolf inside a fence and on display to hundreds of paying customers every day is a poor creature compared to the wolf that might run wild across Rannoch Moor, that patrols a thousand square miles of a Norwegian mountain forest, that leaves a pack in Yellowstone and heads out alone into a landscape 'so inhospitable that it contained not a single track of another animal', apparently to mourn her dead mate, then returns to lead her pack alone on a mission to overpower a neighbouring pack and claim a new territory, that walks 500 miles alone to wind up dead on Interstate 70. Wolves inside a fence are denied – every day of their lives – the right to exercise the imagination wild wolves bring to bear – every day of their lives – on the constantly changing circumstances and challenges of wilderness.

That is a truth apparently lost on Paul Lister, businessman, self-publicist, and – crucially – Highland landowner, whose idea is to fence off 50,000 acres, recreate areas of native woodland inside the fence and reintroduce Scotland's lost mammals, including wolves. The fence is 10 feet high and electric, so there goes anyone's definition of wilderness.

Is it better than a zoo? No.

Is it better than a small zoo? Yes.

Is it still a zoo, nevertheless? Yes.

Would it be possible to get the sense of wolves in a wild landscape from inside the fence? No. A fence, however long, imposes restrictions, and the only thing that a wild wolf permits to impose restrictions on its life is another wolf.

Is it reasonable, or even practicable to expect a wolf pack's idea of its own territory to coincide with Paul Lister's imposed idea? No.

Other questions:

Is there such a thing as a wolf-proof fence? Probably not.

Will the gates in the fence be staffed by marksmen?

If his wolves outsmart his security and escape, will he shoot them?

And is this the only way that wolves will ever come back into Scotland, inside a fence so that there will be no livestock to be harried and no isolated townships living in fear of the sound of a wolf howl, or a glimpse of a shadow moving among shadows at the edge of the trees? So that no-one and no wolf will ever have the opportunity to challenge the medieval character assassination of the wolf that still lives here and there in Europe, and yes, in Britain, in Scotland, in the Highlands?

Is Paul Lister's vision the only socially and politically acceptable solution to the dilemma posed by the very idea of putting wolves back into my native landscape?

No. No, it is emphatically not.

Of all the mountain summits that crowd down on the Glencoe road between Buachaille Etive Mor in the east and Sgurr na Ciche above Loch Leven in the west, none is as unprepossessing, unsung and unloved as Beinn a'Chrulaiste. Its near neighbour across the road is perhaps the most photographed mountain in Scotland, Buachaille Etive Mor, a mountain that so rivets the eye from any direction as to eclipse anything and everything that has the misfortune to fall within its shadow. I am far from immune to its spell myself.

Buachaille (Shepherd)

And at my feet the flotsam
of the moor: the bog triptych
– cotton, myrtle, asphodel –

tormentil, sundew, bluebell,
still-thickening grass, heather, lichen, moss,
unfinished fragrance of orchids.

And glaring down from within
the upgathered robes of Etive
the Shepherd sees my pencil hand
measure a sundew with a thumbnail,
then raise the same thumb
at arm's length to measure
the whole Shepherd from robe-hem
to mountainous brow.

And in the evening the Shepherd
enfolds all that grows within
his sight, and the quiet deer,
eagle, raven, owl, lost wolf howl;
but I remain beyond,
unfolded, and must go on
or coldly wait the dawn.

Besides, Beinn a'Chrulaiste is a mountainous slump, a shrug of a thing, and if you notice it at all, it gives the impression of turning its back on the stupendous pyramidal sculpture of the Shepherd and the serried ridgey glories of Glencoe beyond. But the shrugging one has hidden charms, not the least of which is that you leave behind the Munro-bagging, rock-climbing hordes that torment the Buachaille every day of every year, and the madness of the West Highland Way that plods between the Shrug and the Shepherd, and it is an invariably solitary furrow that you plod up onto the mountain's one thrusting gesture, the outcrop imaginatively called Stob Beinn a'Chrulaiste. It is at this point, a thousand feet above the Glencoe road, that you turn and discover you are looking straight into the Shepherd's navel. The view of Buachaille Etive Mor from high on Beinn a'Chrulaiste, usually seen against the sunlight (unless you are up there very early in the morning) so that Coire na Tulaich and the prow of Stob Dearg are shrouded in the blackest of shadows, confers an alpine glory on the mountain that is not apparent from the road.

Beinn a'Chrulaiste has another distinction in that company, which is a plateau summit. You find yourself drawn to that mountain's way of thinking, and on that airy pedestal, you too turn your back on the Buachaille and the west crammed with mountain ridges, and you sit among ptarmigan and saxifrages and you find yourself facing east, and there at your feet is the whole unfettered miles-wide scope of that magic carpet that is Rannoch Moor, tawny and pale and still winter-weary, grey and blue among the uncounted lochs and lochans and pools and puddles, gold where spotlights of sun fire up the waking land, white where the distant tops are still liberally patched with old snow, the whole thing made mobile by cloud shadows on a southwesterly breeze and the on-off sun that chases in among them. I have been lucky enough to live among the close-gathered mountains and narrow glens of the southmost Highlands for a dozen years now, but sometimes I need something else. I was born and brought up on the east coast at Dundee, with huge skies and sea going horizons uninterrupted by islands and mountains.

Sometimes I go back for that sense of space, to breathe in the salt air I was raised on and to touch old stones and hear the speech of the natives. But sometimes I seek out a different kind of space and I go to Rannoch instead, to the lonely plateau of Beinn a'Chrulaiste that turns its back on Glencoe and stares at the rounded sky and the expansive tracts of Rannoch Moor. It's a freer landscape whose foundation is space, and its air tastes not of North Sea salt but of moor-sweetness. And its speech is not the tongues of the east that I hear in my own head when I go back there, but the gutturals of ptarmigan and red deer and the ragged spring concerto of golden plover and curlew and greenshank, and the once-in-a-while terrier yap of a golden eagle. From any direction you have to climb up onto the moor, for it lies between the 1,000 and 1,500 feet contours and seems to have the muscle to elbow the mountains back in every direction.

My mind is liberated there, and wanders off on new explorations like a Yellowstone wolf hell-bent on the new world of Colorado. So I have returned to the high bright edge of Rannoch Moor, climbed the shrugging mountain, navel-gazed the Buachaille, then climbed onto the plateau where the suddenly revealed moorland sea washes away and away to where Schiehallion stands blue in the east. (From the top of Schiehallion, on the right kind of day, you can see Beinn a'Chrulaiste in the west and Dundee Law in the east. I like to make that kind of connection sometimes, just so that I know I'm standing on solid ground.) I have wolves on my mind, of course, and I remember a famous photograph of a white wolf leaping from an ice-floe, the arc of its leap perfectly reflected in steely water. It must have been reproduced a million times. You can probably buy posters of it everywhere from Alaska to Australia. But my mind is stealing the image and transposing it onto that lochan down there, the one that is roughly the shape of a crab with one claw. But unlike the poster wolf that is frozen forever in mid-air, my Rannoch wolf has hit the ground running, and the slow string of red deer hinds half a mile away is suddenly galvanised. Wolves are running from four different directions, and they turn the deer, and they run alongside them assessing the likeliest target, then they split it from the rest and one wolf leaps for its throat . . .

I remember again the sudden awareness that came my way watching grizzly bears at 20 yards on Kodiak Island, Alaska, a new awareness for me: my species is not the one in charge of this situation. You might imagine – if you have never encountered that awareness before – that it would induce fear. It did no such thing. Instead it was liberating. For the first time in my life (and in my mid-50s, which had been a long time to wait!) I was one creature among countless others with strengths and weaknesses and I shared their landscape, shared their awareness which comes with the proximity of such bears.

If you write about nature for a living, you inevitably strive – and yearn – for an ever greater closeness with your subject, but thousands of years of evolution get in the way, and mostly nature fears your presence in its landscape. It produces a sense of loneliness, at least it does in me, and a powerful and sometimes overbearing sense of regret, redeemed only by extraordinary and isolated moments you have gathered among all the landscapes of your life when some creature takes you at face value and leans towards you. Perhaps an eagle dips a wing and comes to stand on the air 30 feet above you, looking down, making eye contact, assessing you with his dark gold eagle eyes, his wolf-coloured eagle eyes. Perhaps an otter rummages among shoreline rocks, finds you there, and instead of bolting for the safety of the sea, curls up in the sun and watches you watching her. Or a boar badger takes an unexpected turn in his normal route away from the sett and advances along a worn path the width of a single badger through wild hyacinths and wild garlic towards the tree where you stand in shadow imagining yourself to be invisible, and he so disapproves of your scent that he pauses to pee on your boots and ambles off like a wee bear into the dusk. Or you park your car among quiet lochside pines and a chaffinch flies 50 yards to perch on the door mirror of your car and sits there while you lower the window, with a single thought in his head: gimme! And more memorable in my mind than all these, the wild mute swan pen on a Highland loch that sought me out at a low point in her wild life and for ten minutes she slept in my shadow.

Whatever the gesture, whatever the creature, you are made aware of the courage it took, you understand a little better because of the momentary intimacy, and you share nature's comradeship. And on Kodiak Island I became as commonplace as all non-bears, I was suddenly among legions of fellow travellers, the massed ranks of the tribe that defers to bears, and there was no loneliness. And suddenly I too took a bear at face-value and leaned towards her, and who knows, perhaps my leaning assuaged some loneliness in her.

At our best, at our utterly remarkable best, we are capable of reaching out and being accepted by the tribes of nature, even those tribes – like the Kodiak grizzlies – that instil in us in the most unambiguous terms the awareness that we are not in charge of the situation. And even a wolf for whom we are surely the most sworn of enemies, given our mutual history of one-sided slaughter . . . even a wolf will occasionally pause in its daily routine to watch us go by, to stand out in the open at no distance, to watch with an air of frank curiosity that borders on greeting; or it will provide a concert at 200 metres for a man standing naked on his front porch at 3 a.m. on a Norwegian winter's morning.

This is the train of thought that I spill out into the high, cool air above Rannoch Moor, sitting on the plateau summit of Beinn a'Chrulaiste looking east, wondering what it was like after the ice freed it and it grew lightly wooded and the first wolves and bears came prospecting after the first deer – did it look like Yellowstone without the geysers? The first thing I ever read that made me think differently about landscape and wildness and nature came into my mind then, a form of words so familiar to me that I can quote it without looking it up, for it is from the foreword to Gavin Maxwell's *Ring of Bright Water*. There is no one book that I have read more often than that one, the first time 40-something years ago (and how it turned my teenage head!), the most recent time about a month ago:

For I am convinced that man has suffered in his separation from the soil and from the other living creatures of the world; the evolution of his intellect has outrun his needs as an animal and as yet he must still, for security, look on some portion of the earth as it was before he tampered with it.

There is the essence of the argument – to look on some portion of the earth as it was before our species tampered with it. In my own country, that must mean a landscape managed by the wildness of wolves. Yellowstone has shown that it is possible to heal some portion of the earth to something like its old wild self, as it was before we tampered with it. Wilderness *can* be recreated, so long as we don't try and do it ourselves. Wolves provide the best – no, the only – means of restoring something like a native landscape to the natives, both human and non-human. Where I might differ with Gavin Maxwell 50 years after he wrote these words is that 'for security' is no longer the overriding motive. We profess now to know the worth of conservation, of biodiversity, of a landscape replete with native trees as a force for good in the world. We know as indisputable fact that for an ecosystem to perform to its utmost, its top predators must be in place. Yellowstone has reinforced the message for the benefit of those nations of the watching world that remain to be convinced. Regrettably, mine is among those nations.

If we were to introduce a bill to the Scottish Parliament tomorrow to put wolves back into the landscape at Rannoch Moor, centrepiece of the new Heartland National Park, with the safeguard that the Scottish government would permit three wolf packs to establish themselves, and beyond that number take controlling action, following the Norwegian model . . . if we were to do that, there would be vigorous opposition from the predictable sources – the farmers' union, the game-keepers' union, the landowners, probably the anglers, probably hillwalkers' groups. Their arguments are old arguments and they have been defeated in several parts of the world already.

The most frequent objections will centre on the same old fears that emerged from the Dark Ages, and we now know these are groundless. Wolves do not attack people except in circumstances so unusual and so rare that it is impossible to legislate for them, and almost inevitably they result from people tormenting wolves or trying to feed them. Wolves have very good reason to avoid people, a couple of thousand years' worth of reasons. As for wolves killing people, no-one knows when that last happened anywhere in the world, whereas here in Scotland we know for certain that we exterminated them; and whereas here in Scotland we know for certain that at least four children have been killed already this century by their own families' pet dogs.

The price we must pay, and it is the only price we must pay, is to learn that awareness I encountered at the far end of an Alaskan grizzly bear's gaze across 20 yards of fireweed: that situations will exist out there in which your species and mine will not be in charge. You may confidently expect much more thoughtful and considerate responses from reintroduced wild wolves towards your species and mine than our species has shown towards its fellow travellers of the animal kingdom all across the planet, and forever.

The slow string of deer out beyond the lochan shaped like a crab with one claw stops again to browse. No wolf leaps across the mirroring water to disturb their torpor. Like the Yellowstone elk, they have long since forgotten how to behave like red deer. Like the Yellowstone elk they will learn again very quickly once the wolf returns to Rannoch, once they have to share their landscape again with the painter of mountains.

CHAPTER 17
The Last Dream

SHE FELT THE DAWN turn suddenly cold, then she heard swan voices. She crossed a low ridge, a fold in the skin of the Moor, and saw the birds. They were bunched tightly on a lochan, necks tall, calling loudly, staring at the north-west. The water wore that almost-whiteness of the twilit hours, and against it the birds were deep violet. The same shade edged the crests of a thousand wavelets the swans had stirred up in their agitation, as if the surface of the water had caught their mood and determined to share it. They were whooper swans, working north-west up the country before the long flight to Icelandic nesting grounds, stopping off at safe havens their ancestors had used for thousands of years. She knew their voices. The discordant chorus put in her mind the howling of the pack. She became aware again suddenly of her solitude. She knew their loyalty to the same quiet, shallow watersheets among mountains and moors; knew too that they were absent from late spring to early autumn, and that they returned with young birds in their company. That was like the pack returning to a denning site when the new cubs were due.

She also knew they could see beyond the horizon, further than she could see, sensing the approach of storms or other dangers. Now these twelve raised their heads, their vivid yellow bills, and chorused their alarm at what lay in the unseen north-west. She followed their gaze and put her nose to the north-west wind. At last she smelled snow, that sting-in-the-tail snow, that last dance of winter that confounds so many Highland springs.

The swans were further troubled by the appearance of a wolf. None of them had seen a wolf before, yet none was in any doubt about what she was. The spoor and the lessons of their ancestors were everywhere around such quiet waters. Race memory among the creatures of a northern hemisphere wilderness is a silken thread that binds centuries. Much concerning the proximity of wolves is inherited by every new generation, undimmed either by the passage of time or the decline of the wolf on the face of the land. So the swans swam pointedly away to the furthest corner of the lochan, putting a hundred yards of open water between themselves and the shore where the wolf stood. They swam in the same tight group, calling as they swam, reinforcing vigilance in each other and the collective purpose of the group. Then they turned to stare into the north-west again, although never at any moment were fewer than two pairs of eyes delegated to watch the wolf.

She stared too, for curtains of grey-blue, grey-yellow, grey-white, were drawing across the mountains, so that the mountains disappeared eerily by degrees, so that the curtains became advancing waves. Behind the place where the mountains stood, the world was black. She felt the wind grow and grow colder. The first flakes touched her and melted. She watched the swans lie down, breasts pointed to the wind, watched them lay their necks along their spines and pillow their heads deep in sumptuous down and between their hugely folded wings.

She had her own defence against the snow-wind. She lay down, curved her back against it, put her bare nose and furred muzzle between her back legs and swung the thick fur of her tail across her face, and prepared to sit it out, confident in the double luxury of her fur – a dense underfur and an outer layer of long guard hairs. Soon the snow made white ovals of swans and wolf, and a small drift a few inches high built up against her tail. She sighed, and closed her eyes.

The snow eased. She stood and shook herself and the snow slid from her like the shed skin of an adder. The swans lay still as cocoons, all bar one that raised its head a few inches, watching. She saw then that several other furled swans also watched, that for all their restful appearance, they were not at rest, merely still. But she was not interested in the swans. She shook herself again and the snow flew from her like thistledown in a big wind. She raised her own head to scent the air and it smelled of swans and the icy clean edge of the snow wind. She turned a little west of south so that the wind was over her shoulder, so that she could test it as she travelled just by turning her head. She disappeared into the snow-gloom.

Her sudden absence disturbed the swans as much as her sudden presence had done. They rose on the water and flexed their wings, shouldered away the snow from their plumage, then gathered loudly and swam into a tight wedge of birds. The wolf could be anywhere, could come at them in a sudden bounding run. Their heads jerked on tall necks, their voices rose, a discordant woodwind fanfare. (They had this in common with the wolf pack when they gave voice: if a note of true harmony was inadvertently struck by two voices, one of them changed pitch at once.) One swan, the self-appointed decision-maker, leaned his neck at the wind, dead straight, brought his wings up above the top of his back and pulled them down hard until the tips of his primary feathers flipped back off the surface of the water. That single wing-beat lifted his entire body clear of the water, and as it lifted he began to run. Running and flying at once, he led the swans into the loud, urgent grace of take-off. Almost at once the swans, too, were lost to the curtained folds of snow, their voices quietening into unseen distance. They flew blind and unerringly into the grey-white north-west.

The lochan subsided and grew still, a slate-grey silence on the whitened Moor. The snow eased but still fell. The evidence that swan and wolf had lingered there also began to disappear. The swans had a sure journey, a known destination. The wolf had neither. But the Wolf Wind had come with the snow, and she felt for the first time since the killing of her pack that she might be within dreaming reach of other wolves. So she travelled in search of a dreaming place. She travelled more or less south because she had fled the killing of her pack that way, because nothing had persuaded her to change direction, because she had found the ancient refuge of

Rannoch. If she found other wolves, if a new beginning was possible, she would lead them back there, back to the difficult place among rocks in the Black Wood of Rannoch, back to the fraternal embrace of the pines. It could begin again there.

She travelled all that day with the same easy lope, the wolf's long-distance gait. She rose and fell with the contours of the moor where it heaved in waves and troughs, the old spoor of the Great Ice. Distance was her destination. The solitary snow-furrow of her footfall showed the evenness of her stride. Nothing distracted her from the pursuit of distance. The other creatures of the moor who saw her coming or scented her steady downwind advance gave her room. There was nothing to be gained by intruding on the forced march of a wolf through their territories, not for any of them, whatever their size and numbers and tenacity and courage. They all fell back, made way, and sensed relief when she passed without pause or sideways glance.

Hours devoured miles, until at last she began to slow and take note of the landscape again. The snow had stopped, and spring sunlight forced the clouds further and further up mountainsides, revealing piece by piece the mountain wall that signalled the southern edge of the moor. At the west end of that wall, the composite mass of Beinn a' Chreachain and Beinn Achaladair emerged in the aftermath of the storm bloated with snow. She judged the narrow glen down their eastern flanks too difficult in those conditions. The snow had funnelled there and drifted to impassable depths. She chose instead the headwaters of the Tulla Water, saw the river grow and head south-west on easier, lower ground. She would keep its company at least as far as the mountains' western flanks; there she hoped for an easier route to the south again. She fell in with the river and her new course, and resumed the same travelling rhythm as before, closing with every loping stride the distance between herself and the bidding of the Wolf Wind. Then she saw pine trees.

After the wild, bare, arduous, snow-deep moor and the looming bulk of the mountains, the sudden distant appearance of Loch Tulla, blue and sunlit, and a new thickening of pine trees beyond reinforced her trust in the beckoning of the Wolf Wind. Miles fell before her, overpowered by her strength, stamina, resolve, and her sense of purpose that was nothing less than life itself, life for all wolves. Evening sun pushed the shadows of the trees out towards her in welcome. She reached the first tree and rubbed her flank joyously against it. She found a patch of bare heather and blae-berry leaves under the canopy of a greater tree where almost no snow had penetrated. She squirmed and rolled in the fragrant understorey of the forest. Every mile since she had left the swans at the lochan, every stride of every mile had been snowbound to the ankle or to the knee. Now she writhed like a cub in the snowless green. She was back among brother pines, like the pines that had shaded and scented her earliest days in Strathspey, and in the fraternal embrace of pines she felt at ease again.

She walked slower, deep into the trees, found a patch of new grass yellowed by the evening sun, curved her spine down into it, wrapped her tail over her face and closed her eyes. Her heaving flank slowed into a settled rhythm. She summoned one last dream and sent it away across the forest, a wolf track that left no footprint.